Meditations for
The Twelve Steps—
A Spiritual Journey

Friends in Recovery
with Jerry S.

RECOVERY PUBLICATIONS, INC.
San Diego

Meditations for

THE

TWELVE

STEPS—A

SPIRITUAL

JOURNEY

Published by Recovery Publications, Inc.
1201 Knoxville Street
San Diego, CA 92110-3718
(619) 275-1350

Library of Congress Cataloging-in-Publication Data
Friends in Recovery.
Meditations for the twelve steps : a spritual journey / Friends in
Recovery with Jerry S.
p.   cm.
ISBN 0-941405-21-4
1. Twelve-step programs—Religious aspects—Meditations.
I. Jerry S.   II. Title.
BL624.5.F75   1993
242'.4—dc20   *92-42896*
                                                          CIP

All the scripture quotations are from the New International Version
of the Bible.

The names and identifying details of most of the individuals whose
stories are shared in these meditations are changed. Where the
names are not changed, the stories are used with permission from
the individuals.

The Twelve Steps are reprinted with permission of Alcoholics
Anonymous World Services, Inc. Permission to reprint this material
does not mean that AA has reviewed or approved the contents of this
publication, nor that AA agrees with the views expressed herein.
AA is a program of recovery from alcoholism only—use of the Twelve
Steps in connection with programs and activities which are patterned
after AA, but which address other problems, does not imply otherwise.

Printed in the United States of America
First edition
10 9 8 7 6 5 4 3 2 1

Introduction

*T*he Twelve-Step program is not a human-powered program. God is the source of our power and our growth. Therefore, daily contact with God is all-important. The Twelve-Step program is a spiritual but not a religious program. God makes himself known to us through the Twelve Steps without any religious effort on our part.

Our spiritual journey begins with our acknowledgment of powerlessness. We learn through the pain and unmanageability of our lives that we cannot control our lives or the lives of others. Under our own management, our lives have failed, not prospered. In Step One, we admit this understanding.

After Step One, we are left rather empty and wanting. That's where God comes in. In Step Two, we begin to exercise faith—faith that God provides. We simply believe that a power greater than ourselves can restore us to sanity (and take care of us). We needn't even put a name on God in Step Two. We simply exercise that bud of faith that God is causing to grow in our hearts.

In Step Three, we come to a place of decision, not action. We decide to turn our will and our lives over to the care of God as we are growing to understand him. This decision will, by itself, create a new serenity in our lives, and it will prepare us for the introspective action of Step Four.

Step Four asks us to make a searching and fearless moral inventory of ourselves. In this step, God helps us search our hearts and lives for those defects, shortcomings, and failures that have marked our lives up until this time. This inventory lists more than our failures and sins. It lists our survival techniques—our dysfunctional attempts at living. Step Four also provides for a positive inventory. We list our positive traits and our strengths, which God will transform and use. This is often more difficult than listing our faults.

Step Five requires confession. We admit to God, ourselves, and another human being the exact nature of the wrongs we listed in Step Four. God aids us in this process of becoming vulnerable, and if we ask for his help, he directs us to the right person.

Willingness is a state of mind and heart, and we must arrive at that place. Step Six acknowledges this. The earlier steps, especially Steps Four and Five, have made us acutely aware of our need to change. And now Step Six gives us the time and opportunity to recognize and collect our willingness to move on to the work of change that still lies ahead.

Humility is also a state of mind and heart. But more, it is the spirit that controls the rest of our spiritual journey, a journey that humbly relies on God and that humbly faces those we've damaged and offended. In Step Seven we come to God, not to confess, but to ask. We tried to change, we determined to do better, but we always failed. The time has come to ask, to humbly ask God to remove what we cannot remove: our sins, our shortcomings.

Step Eight provides a time for reflection. Like Step Six, it gives us time to recognize and collect our willingness to move on. But unlike Step Six, Step Eight asks us to make a list of the persons we have harmed. As the names and faces of friends, family, enemies, associates, and others come before us, we must be ever vigilant to remember that the program is about us, not them. Many of the people we recall and list have hurt and damaged us, too. But we are working our program, not theirs. If we ask, God will help us to see these people from his perspective, not ours. And God will nurture the willingness to make the amends that Step Nine requires.

Step Nine calls for action. It also calls for courage. Many agree that this is the most difficult step, but many also agree that it is the most powerful one. Step Nine allows us to make a significant and lasting break from our past behavior. Step Nine enables us to separate ourselves from the mistakes of our past. And Step Nine is for us—first and foremost.

The first of the maintenance steps is Step Ten. This step begins to teach us a way of life that will keep us from falling back into past mistakes or old habit patterns. Step Ten encourages us to examine ourselves daily, and it encourages us to make prompt confessions and amends. The prompt recognition, admission, and correction of our moral defects will ensure a life-style that fosters recovery and health.

Step Eleven is another maintenance step; it keeps us in touch with God. We develop prayer, meditation, and a God-consciousness that help control our daily living. We understand that God is not there to be manipulated or controlled. Prayer is not our opportunity to tell God how to run our lives or his world. Prayer is a time to connect with God. God already has a wonderful plan for our lives; we must ask him what that plan is and ask him for the strength to accomplish his will.

Step Twelve acknowledges that the Twelve-Step program is, indeed, a spiritual journey. Working the program provides a spiritual awakening as we are called back to the basic principles of the kingdom of God. But more than mere acknowledgment, there is a mission encapsulated in Step Twelve—that we share this spiritual program with others and that we demonstrate the principles of the program through our everyday living.

The Twelve-Step program, this spiritual journey, is a way of life, a way of recovery, and a way of revelation as God's life is seen through his people. May God bless us as we employ these principles, may God enable us to work the steps for our good, may God reveal himself to us through his Word and Spirit, may God encourage us through our participation in meetings, and may we act upon God's grace for his glory's sake. Amen!

A NOTE BEFORE BEGINNING

This book of meditations was written as a companion to *The Twelve Steps—A Spiritual Journey* (Recovery Publications, Inc., 1988), and each meditation corresponds to a Scripture verse found in the respective chapter/step of that workbook. For that reason, there are as few as nine meditations for some steps and as many as twelve meditations for others.

Our hope is that this book of meditations will provide a source of illustration and inspiration for those who face the serious issues addressed in the workbook. Those who have already worked through the workbook are encouraged to go through it again with the meditations. You may find it helpful to respond to the questions again using a different color ink and dating each new written entry. Whether or not you have worked *The Twelve Steps—A Spiritual Journey,* this book can work for you.

This book is intended to help you personally identify with the questions, issues, and principles that are incorporated in daily work of *The Twelve Steps—A Spiritual Journey.* Hence, the stories often reflect the personal experiences of someone in the program. Also, the meditations are intended as a tool to help develop the habit of daily Scripture reading, meditation, and prayer.

The Twelve Steps and Related Scripture

STEP ONE: *We admitted we were powerless over the effects of our separation from God—that our lives had become unmanageable.*
I know nothing good lives in me, that is, in my sinful nature. For I have the desire to do what is good, but I cannot carry it out. (Romans 7:18)

STEP TWO: *Came to believe that a power greater than ourselves could restore us to sanity.*
For it is God who works in you to will and to act according to his good purpose. (Philippians 2:13)

STEP THREE: *Made a decision to turn our will and our lives over to the care of God as we understood him.*
Therefore, I urge you, brothers, in view of God's mercy, to offer your bodies as living sacrifices, holy and pleasing to God—which is your spiritual worship. (Romans 12:1)

STEP FOUR: *Made a searching and fearless moral inventory of ourselves.*
Let us examine our ways and test them, and let us return to the Lord. (Lamentations 3:40)

STEP FIVE: *Admitted to God, to ourselves, and to another human being the exact nature of our wrongs.*
Therefore confess your sins to each other and pray for each other so that you may be healed. (James 5:16a)

STEP SIX: *Were entirely ready to have God remove all these defects of character.*
Humble yourself before the Lord, and he will lift you up. (James 4:10)

STEP SEVEN: Humbly asked him to remove our shortcomings.
If we confess our sins, he is faithful and just and will forgive us our sins and purify us from all unrighteousness. (1 John 1:9)

STEP EIGHT: Made a list of all persons we had harmed and became willing to make amends to them all.
Do to others as you would have them do to you. (Luke 6:31)

STEP NINE: Made direct amends to such people wherever possible, except when to do so would injure them or others.
Therefore, if you are offering your gift at the altar and there remember that your brother has something against you, leave your gift there in front of the altar. First go and be reconciled to your brother; then come and offer your gift. (Matthew 5:23–24)

STEP TEN: Continued to take personal inventory and, when we were wrong, promptly admitted it.
So, if you think you are standing firm, be careful that you don't fall. (1 Corinthians 10:12)

STEP ELEVEN: Sought through prayer and meditation to improve our conscious contact with God as we understood him, praying only for knowledge of his will for us and the power to carry that out.
Let the word of Christ dwell in you richly. (Colossians 3:16a)

STEP TWELVE: Having had a spiritual awakening as the result of these steps, we tried to carry this message to others, and to practice these principles in all our affairs.
Brothers, if someone is caught in a sin, you who are spiritual should restore him gently. But watch yourself, or you also may be tempted. (Galatians 6:1)

STEP ONE

We admitted we were powerless over the effects of our separation from God—that our lives had become unmanageable.

I am worn out from groaning; all night long I flood my bed with weeping and drench my couch with tears. My eyes grow weak with sorrow; they fail because of all my foes. *(Ps. 6:6–7)*

Step One Reflections

As we approach Step One, we need to remember something about God—he alone is the all-powerful one. God does all things perfectly. We do not.

Throughout the pages of the Bible, God has sought to show his people how powerless we are in ourselves and how much we need his intervention and help. God called Abraham to be the father of many nations, and then he gave him a barren wife. God called Moses to lead his people to a promised land, and then he made him wander in a desert for forty years. God called Gideon to defeat the Midianites, and then God took away Gideon's army and its weapons. God called the Virgin Mary to be the mother of the Messiah, and then he gave her no husband.

In every case, God's people cried out to him in their powerlessness. They wanted to obey God's call on their lives, but they were totally unable to fullfil it. The effect of their separation from God was impotence, unmanageability, and frustration.

The same is true for us. We know that God has given us life, and we long to make something of it. But we are powerless. In our own strength and control, life has been unfulfilled. We have lived in the illusion of control. We thought that we were able to manage our lives, but our efforts have brought only pain. Like a patient who tries to perform surgery on him- or herself, we have tried to fix our lives. But the fixing only creates greater harm, not healing.

For most of us, even the thought of starting this program seems beyond us. We've had so much failure and so many failed self-surgeries that we are at our wit's end. But that's okay. That realization is the beginning of healing. God has brought us to that understanding. It's God's job to dispel the illusions we live in. It's our job to admit our powerlessness when he does.

Step One: We admitted we were powerless over the effects of our separation from God—that our lives had become unmanageable.

Scripture: I am worn out from groaning; all night long I flood my bed with weeping and drench my couch with tears. My eyes grow weak with sorrow; they fail because of all my foes. (Ps. 6:6–7)

The hardest I ever cried in my life was when a close friend died. He had been like a father. Things were forever changed. I was empty, angry, and lost. But I was also powerless to change the accident at the bridge.

I don't suppose I felt anything near that helplessness and loss until the day I faced myself in Step One. God opened my eyes to see myself. He showed me how utterly powerless I was to change my life or my behavior. With that revelation, I lost someone very important. I lost myself. Flawed as I was, the old me was all I had. But God had stripped me by opening my eyes. I could no longer manage and control life. My old ways only brought me pain. I needed to change, but I didn't know how.

For a long time after that, I didn't want to go out in public. I didn't want to make the same old mistakes. But I didn't know how to live differently. I was lost and empty. It seemed that the only thing I was good at now was crying and slobbering. I did lots of that. I had said "I'm sorry" to many people many times, but I usually said it to control them. Now, I really was sorry. Deep in my gut I felt remorse and loss.

I can't report any magic cures or change. But I know the simple admission of my powerlessness was a major achievement. My friend is gone forever, and so is the old me.

God, help me admit that the old me needs to die.

Step One: We admitted we were powerless over the effects of our separation from God—that our lives had become unmanageable.

Scripture: This day I call heaven and earth as witnesses against you that I have set before you life and death, blessings and curses. Now choose life, so that you and your children may live and that you may love the Lord your God, listen to his voice, and hold fast to him. (Deut. 30:19-20)

Some time ago I accompanied a friend and his two boys to "The Happiest Place on Earth"—Disneyland! This wonderful place is also known by another name, the Magic Kingdom. Within this kingdom, which Walt built, there is beauty, fantasy, fun, and, most of all, order. Life is so wonderful at Disneyland because it was built and still is run according to Walt's plan.

During that visit I was enchanted by the Magic Kingdom, but only on the surface. I found that inside myself I was untouched by its joy. I was standing within the gates of the happiest place on earth, but I wasn't happy. By trying to control my life, I had made a mess of things. All I could do was confess my powerlessness and unmanageability.

In my sinfulness, I have abused the precious life entrusted to me. God provided a plan for blessed living, but I chose my own distorted plan. With my self-rule came the curse, which is nothing more than the natural consequence of my sin. I sowed control and self-will, and I reaped sorrow and pain.

I don't know about you, but my self-rule has brought me nothing but pain. I long to know a happy kingdom inside.

God, help me admit that you have a plan for my life that's better than my own.

Step One: We admitted we were powerless over the effects of our separation from God—that our lives had become unmanageable.

Scripture: The man who thinks he knows something does not yet know as he ought to know. (1 Cor. 8:2)

*H*ave you ever had to pick a horse from the stable? On my last trip, the stable hand asked what level of rider I was. I said, "Expert!" I didn't think I had lied since I often rode old Mitzy back on the farm. Of course Mitzy was a hundred horse-years old and asleep during most of my rides. Nevertheless, she took me at my word and headed back into the stable.

When the hand reemerged from the barn, she was leading a spirited stallion named Nitro! She said, "He's hard to handle, but I'm sure you can manage him." In less than an hour, I was in an ambulance with a seriously injured back!

I often approach the rest of my life the way I approached that ill-fated ride. "Mr. Know-It-All" can handle just about everything and everyone. But the truth is that I am just a scared kid who wants to seem important by being in control. However, life doesn't work with me in control, and I don't even know that until I'm down. God and life know how to pull the rug (or horse) out from underneath me. But when I'm down, it's for revelation, not humiliation.

Just the other day my daughter asked, "Do you know how to ride horses, Dad?" I answered, "I used to know how, but after a fall, I forgot everything I knew."

God, help me admit what I don't know.

Step One: *We admitted we were powerless over the effects of our separation from God—that our lives had become unmanageable.*

Scripture: *That day when evening came, he said to his disciples, "Let us go over to the other side." Leaving the crowd behind, they took him along, just as he was, in the boat. A furious squall came up, and the waves broke over the boat, so that it was nearly swamped. Jesus was in the stern, sleeping on a cushion. The disciples woke him and said to him, "Teacher, don't you care if we drown?" He got up, rebuked the wind and said to the waves, "Quiet! Be still." Then the wind died down and it was completely calm. He said to his disciples, "Why are you so afraid? Do you still have no faith?" They were terrified and asked each other, "Who is this? Even the wind and the waves obey him."* (Mark 4:35–41)

I'm sure you've known the sort of person with whom you feel you're completely safe—when you're with that person, nothing bad can happen. A man I'll call Boats, a retired Navy commander who had served on battleships in olden days, was like that for me. Boats was my sailing instructor. He taught me the ways of the wind, the dangers of the sea, and the inerrant principles of sailing. "When you're in trouble," he used to say, "just let go of everything—the tiller and the sheet. The boat will right itself, trust me." He boasted that no student had ever capsized a boat while he was in it. If the boat was in trouble, he would slap my hands to make me let go. So I kept his record intact. I knew for a fact that, with him, the boat was unsinkable.

In recovery, I am learning a similar principle. My fear and lack of trust cause me to hang on to the controls, but my safety is in letting go. I could not right my own life. It had capsized many times with me at the helm, and I lived in a constant state of panic and fear. But as I admit my powerlessness and let go, my life is steadied.

Well, one day Boats made me go solo. I had to sail without him, and I got wet. I couldn't let go of the sheet.

God, teach me to let go.

Step One: *We admitted we were powerless over the effects of our separation from God—that our lives had become unmanageable.*

Scripture: *"I am the true vine and my Father is the gardener. He cuts off every branch in me that bears no fruit, while every branch that does bear fruit he trims clean so that it will be even more fruitful."* *(John 15:1–2)*

I took a big risk by going to the men's retreat. I was on a church-sponsored sabbatical for burn-out, and I hated being around people, especially church people. I found it nearly impossible to socialize. So I often walked or prayed alone in isolated areas of the retreat center.

During one of my alone times, something I hated even worse than church people approached me—a cat. I'm sure cats are great creatures, but I just don't like them. They're not very friendly to me. But this particular cat jumped right into my lap and began to arch his back for petting, purring and begging for attention. I told him that I did not want company, and I especially didn't want a cat. But he didn't seem to understand. He continued to purr and arch and beg for attention. I was eventually overtaken by a strong urge to pet him. He loved it.

After a few moments of petting this scruffy but adoring creature, I began to think about other creatures I disliked—like church people. I wondered if I would ever be rid of the hate and bitterness I felt in my heart. I knew I was supposed to love others but I had no power or will to do it. All I knew was that God knew my hurt, and he alone is able to trim such things from my life.

God, I have no power over the way I feel about certain people.

Step One: We admitted we were powerless over the effects of our separation from God—that our lives had become unmanageable.

Scripture: When he came to his senses, he said, "How many of my father's hired men have food to spare, and here I am starving to death!" (Luke 15:17)

One Saturday morning, five-year-old Rex was upset. His family had conspired against him. And when he couldn't watch his favorite Saturday morning cartoons, he decided to run away. He packed a peanut butter sandwich inside a pair of underwear and slung it over a stick like a kid on television. Then he was off. When he was about half a mile away and just across from the supermarket, he decided to eat. The sandwich was really dry, and he hadn't thought to bring water. Suddenly he started to panic. Without water to wash it down, the peanut butter might turn to cement in his throat and not make it to his stomach!

Just then Rex's mom pulled out of the supermarket's parking lot. She'd almost reached home before it dawned on her that the little boy across from the store was her son. When she finally pulled alongside of Rex, she found him hysterical and crying out for her. He held her tighter than he ever had, and when he felt safe, he said, "I would have come home someday, Mom. I'm just a kid, you know."

Like our little prodigal, no matter how self-sufficient we act, we are really powerless kids in need of our Father's love and care. We may think we are in control when we stage our dramatic exploits, but you can't argue when life's peanut butter is stuck in your throat.

God, I can't live life on my own.

Step One: We admitted we were powerless over the effects of our separation from God—that our lives had become unmanageable.

Scripture: *"I know that nothing good lives in me, that is, in my sinful nature. For I have the desire to do what is good, but I cannot carry it out. Now if I do what I do not want to do, it is no longer I who do it, but it is sin living in me that does it." (Rom. 7:18–20)*

*F*rom early childhood, I have had dreams about flying. In my dreams, I freely soar over housetops, high-voltage wires, trees, and all my cares. But when the dream ends, so does my freedom and power of flight. Reality sets in, and I remember my life—all the troubles, problems, and pains that drag me back down to earth. I'd love to soar above my failings and sins, but I can't. My sinful nature holds me like gravity.

Sin is a spiritual reality, and we're all affected by the law of sin. I am not bad, but the sin that has power over me is. Sin holds me captive to a life that is powerless and unmanageable. I'd love to soar above its effect, but that's simply not possible.

But once I admit that I am powerless and my life is unmanageable, another law can emerge: God's grace. Just as the law of aerodynamics can overcome the law of gravity, the law of God's mercy and grace can set me free from sin and its effects. I know I can't fly. I also know I can't overcome sin's effect or have life in my control. Yet, as surely as the liberating law of aerodynamics allows airplanes to overcome gravity, there is hope that sin's effect will be overcome once I admit my powerlessness.

God, I feel so heavy from sin's effect.

Step One: *We admitted we were powerless over the effects of our separation from God—that our lives had become unmanageable.*

Scripture: *But he said to me, "My grace is sufficient for you, for my power is made perfect in weakness." Therefore I will boast all the more gladly about my weaknesses, so that Christ's power may rest on me. That is why, for Christ's sake, I delight in weaknesses, in insults, in hardships, in persecutions, in difficulties. For when I am weak, then I am strong. (2 Cor. 12:9–10)*

The man seated next to me was a stranger. We were listening to a strict and authoritarian preacher at a men's retreat. The preacher admonished us to become disciplined, pick ourselves up, control our lives and families, be in charge! When the sermon was done, I knew I was uncomfortable with its message, but the man next to me was fidgeting and mumbling to himself. I learned that he was a well-educated professional but, also, a recovering drug abuser in a Twelve-Step program. With hopeless resignation he shook his head and said, "I can't do what that man said. I have no discipline. I'm too weak!"

I said, "Good! You could never generate enough strength to please yourself or God." I reminded him of Step One and said, "Your best place is powerlessness before God. Only when you give up solving your problems, can God start. Our human flesh and old nature feels good 'doing something.' As long as we are 'doing,' we feel in control and in charge, but we are *not* in recovery. Recovery requires surrender, not more discipline."

My new friend and I skipped that preacher's next sermon. We were weak enough.

God, help me not be afraid of my weakness.

Step One: We admitted we were powerless over the effects of our separation from God—that our lives had become unmanageable.

Scripture: He who trusts in himself is a fool, but he who walks in wisdom is kept safe. (Prov. 28:26)

When I was in high school I asked my dad if I could smoke. He said no. I asked him if I could quit school and join the Navy early. He said no. I asked him if I could hitchhike to New Orleans. He said no. I asked if I could have a motorcycle. He said no. I couldn't understand why he was so unreasonable and mean-spirited. Jeepers, I just wanted to be like other guys and enjoy life!

Well, today I have a different opinion about my dad's guidance and counsel. All my old friends who smoked now wish that they hadn't. My high school diploma allowed me access to an advanced electronics school in the Navy. And while a chaplain for the Los Angeles Sheriff, I saw the bloodied and broken remains of many motorcyclists and witnessed one boy die before my eyes. Dad wasn't really so stupid after all. I'm glad I obeyed (most of the time).

I had to abandon many juvenile plans as I grew up. And today I find that there are still illusions to be cast off. My biggest fallacy is that I can run my own life.

By the way, I asked God if I could be in control. He said no. But he said I could see New Orleans someday.

God, it's not easy letting go of illusions.

STEP TWO

Came to believe that a power greater than ourselves could restore us to sanity.

*F*or it is God who works in you to will and to act according to his good purpose. *(Phil. 2:13)*

Step Two Reflections

In Step Two we begin to reflect upon our Higher Power, we remember that God has always accomplished the impossible for his people. He has restored and redeemed people in bondage, people in fear, people in weakness, and people in great hopelessness. The principle of Step One puts us in a perfect place for Step Two—a place of powerlessness.

The nation of Israel began from the barren womb of Sarah. Israel was led out of Egyptian bondage by Moses, a man filled with fear and self-doubt. God delivered his people from the Philistines' tyranny and Goliath's threats by using a little shepherd boy, David. And when his people needed a savior, God brought about his plan through a poor, teenaged girl named Mary, a virgin. Just as God planted the seed for a savior in Mary's virgin womb, he plants the seeds of recovery and restoration in our powerless hearts. And just as Mary needed no man to bring forth the miracle, God needs no help from us. God acts upon the smallest hint of faith in our hearts—faith that he gives.

With faith in our hearts, we are able to exchange what we believe is sane behavior for what God believes is sane behavior. We have believed that it is sane to take personal control of our lives and our destiny. But God tells us that it is sane to release our control. We have always believed that it is sane to trust only ourselves. But God tells us that it is sane to trust only him. We have believed that it is sane to fix ourselves. But God tells us that it is sane to entrust our recovery to him.

Remember how the nation of Israel felt sane and secure in Egypt? But in Egypt they were in slavery and bondage. God told them that it was more sane and secure to enter the desert with him. In the same way, we have actually felt sane and secure in our old patterns, habits, and dysfunction—in our old bondage. But the faith that God provides will help us see sanity from God's perspective. His faith will enable us to let go of old thought patterns and to trust his ways.

Simply believe that God is and that he is able to restore us to sanity. Let us respond the way Mary responded to the angel who told her of God's plan. Mary simply answered, "May it be to me as you have said."

Step Two: Came to believe that a power greater than ourselves could restore us to sanity.

Scripture: Immediately Jesus made the disciples get into the boat and go on ahead of him to the other side. . . . but the boat was . . . buffeted by the waves. . . . During the fourth watch of the night Jesus went out to them, walking on the lake. . . . "Lord, if it's you," Peter replied, "tell me to come to you on the water." "Come," he said. Then Peter got down out of the boat and walked on the water to Jesus. But when he saw the wind, he was afraid and, beginning to sink, cried out, "Lord, save me!" Immediately Jesus reached out his hand and caught him. "You of little faith," he said, "why did you doubt?" And when they climbed into the boat, the wind died down. (Matt. 14:22–32)

We were visiting Uncle Carl, who lived on a lake. I played on the boat dock while Dad and Carl talked on the shore. As I tried to step from one floating dock to another, I fell in between. I still remember the emerald-green turbulence and bubbles that accompanied my plunge. Amazingly, I wasn't afraid, although I was too small to swim. Suddenly, I saw an arm—Dad's. Although the water was over my head, I was within Dad's reach.

I have come to believe that my heavenly Father is able to rescue me as well. I may venture out in water that is over my head, but I believe that I am always within his reach. I can't explain it to you, but I'm not afraid. I've seen his arm reach out.

It is important to know that God rescues us and miraculously delivers us, not because we deserve it nor because we have somehow earned it. God rescues us and cares for us only because of his love and grace. God loves us. All he asks in return is that we believe in that love and accept it. And in believing we stay well within his reach no matter what storm life brings.

Heavenly Father, I believe I'm within your reach.

***Step Two: Came to believe that a power greater than ourselves
could restore us to sanity.***

Scripture: *He replied, "Because you have so little faith, I tell you the
truth, if you have faith as small as a mustard seed, you can say to this
mountain, 'Move from here to there' and it will move. Nothing will be
impossible for you." (Matt. 17:20)*

*F*or eight years I took very strong and
addictive painkillers, muscle relaxers, and pills to sleep at night.
The trouble and stress of life kept me tense and in pain. The pills
kept the edge off my pain and dulled my life. Yet my way of cop-
ing brought a different pain: the judgment of family and friends.
"Stop taking all those pills!" they preached. "You'll kill yourself."
What they didn't know was that I wanted to die. I was tired of
pain and living out of control. If all the pills didn't kill me, I
feared some hideous disease would. I hated living like this, but
try as I might, I couldn't change. I was insane.

I can't explain how things changed. One day, I just gave up
trying. In my prayer journal I actually wrote, "I quit!" That's all
I entered for that date. The next morning deep in my heart there
was a tiny glimmer, just a hint of hope. I had been given something I could not produce on my own: faith. Suddenly, I began to
believe that God could help me. That's all. But it was the beginning of my recovery.

Faith is a gift. And even the smallest seed of faith can start a
miracle. I gave God my pills, and he gave me a seed.

God, my pain is like a mountain. Please move it.

Step Two: Came to believe that a power greater than ourselves could restore us to sanity.

Scripture: "'If you can'?" said Jesus. "Everything is possible for him who believes." Immediately the boy's father exclaimed, "I do believe; help me overcome my unbelief!" (Mark 9:23–24)

I have a friend who is a fire-and-brimstone preacher. He roasts the sinners every Sunday. I love him, but I find it very hard to listen to his preaching. He practices what I call "magic Christianity." He believes and teaches that if you say the right words and prayers and promises, God *must* answer. But I'm afraid he's trying to control God like he does his children and congregation. Sorry.

One day the magic didn't work. It hadn't for years, but he woke up. The pain woke him up. His wife was seriously ill, and he suddenly found that God was deaf. The spells didn't work. And he came to me. I told him that he needed a new God like mine, which I found in the Bible. I told him that my God is sovereign and doesn't do what I tell him to do. Instead, I lay my life before God every day and ask him what he wants me to do.

I had to learn that I can't control my life and I certainly can't control God. Once I surrendered and admitted my powerlessness (even over God), I found the strength and faith I needed to find sanity. I also found a new God, a God who does miracles on his terms, not mine.

My friend couldn't receive what I had to say. He is very hollow and empty inside. And although he preaches to many, he is very far from God.

Sovereign God, I don't want to control you, I want to believe.

Step Two: ***Came to believe that a power greater than ourselves could restore us to sanity.***

Scripture: *The Lord is close to the brokenhearted and saves those who are crushed in spirit. A righteous man may have many troubles, but the Lord delivers him from them all; he protects all his bones, not one of them will be broken. Evil will slay the wicked; the foe of the righteous will be condemned. The Lord redeems his servants; no one who takes refuge in him will be condemned. (Ps. 34:18–22)*

*R*ecently I received this letter from an adult child. With her permission, I share it: "I've been depressed the last couple of days. It seems like all the joy in my life has gone. I don't know how long it's going to take me to get out of this mood. All I know is that I can't control it. I've just given it to God. Something reminded me of a very unpleasant anniversary. It was eighteen years ago this week that my first husband killed himself. And even though my conscious mind didn't want to deal with this painful memory, my subconscious still tormented me.

"Looking back, I can recall the helplessness of my situation. It seemed like everyone enjoyed taking advantage of a widow who was in shock and numb. Or else they analyzed his suicide and made me feel guilty. Damn them! But somehow my spirit knew then that God had never left my side. He gave me the strength and courage to carry on. I believed that God was the only one who understood and shared my pain, and that meant a lot.

"Even if the pain returns once a year to remind me of my helplessness in life, I am also reminded with joy of God's love and compassion for me."

Believing in a Higher Power doesn't exempt us from sadness. But it gives us someone to share it with.

God above, be near.

Step Two: Came to believe that a power greater than ourselves could restore us to sanity.

Scripture: *Indeed, in our hearts we felt the sentence of death. But this happened that we might not rely on ourselves but on God, who raises the dead. (2 Cor. 1:9)*

Can God raise the dead? I've become convinced that he can. When I first started attending Twelve-Step meetings, I was impressed by the number of times participants spoke about death. Some had attempted suicide in their insanity, others had plotted murder, still more said they lived with a death wish. Almost everyone knew someone who had been killed because of chemical abuse or domestic violence.

Thoughts of death were not foreign to me. I knew what it was like to feel so much pain and internal agony that death seemed like a better option. But these people who spoke of death all had another thing in common: God or their Higher Power. Some who had even claimed to be atheists or agnostics said, "God made himself known to me and did what I could not do for myself." The meetings were filled with talk about a loving and forgiving God, a God full of grace, who was able to do the impossible.

Just the other day, I sat and prayed with a mother whose daughter is near death because of her own abusive and insane compulsion. With tears she said, "She's beyond help and has one foot in the grave." I thought of the many people I know who would disagree. They would tell this mother that God can even raise the dead—they're living proof.

God of life, raise me from my insanity and death.

Step Two: Came to believe that a power greater than ourselves could restore us to sanity.

Scripture: For it is God who works in you to will and to act according to his good purpose. (Phil. 2:13)

*O*ver the years, my family and I have often visited a popular local beach community. We go there to shop or to see the sights. But for as long as I can remember, the state highway through town has been dug up, detoured, or destroyed. It has been a nightmare to drive through town. But worse, none of the road construction has ever made sense. My wife and I have asked the same question for years: What in the world are they doing?

Just last weekend we visited the beach community again. We were surprised to find the highway open. To our amazement, the city streets, which used to cross the highway, now went under it. But the city streets were not just underpasses; they were ornate tunnels that emerged from under the new freeway to beautiful vistas of the ocean. I could have never imagined this wonderful outcome and result. Suddenly, it made sense.

Our lives are much the same way. During our recovery, all we seem to see is the evidence of construction. Our lives are dug up, detoured, and, apparently, destroyed. All this construction and work can be depressing until we remember that God is the one doing the work, and he has a wonderful plan. He sees the end result when all we see is demolition and detour. During these times we need to remember that God is in control of our reconstruction, and he has a beautiful plan.

God, help me remember that you are at work in my life and that your plan is good.

Step Two: *Came to believe that a power greater than ourselves could restore us to sanity.*

Scripture: *Not that we are competent to claim anything for ourselves, but our competence comes from God. (2 Cor. 3:5)*

*C*odependents—like me—tend to do a lot of fishing. You see, I never thought much of myself. So, I fish for compliments. "Boy, am I stupid," I might say. Then I wait for someone to respond, "Oh, no you're not." I then feign humility and say, "Really?" Or at other times, I might ask, "Jeepers, am I ugly and fat or what?" Then in silent desperation I wait for someone to make me feel better about myself. But you know what? Even if they told me everything I wanted to hear, I wouldn't believe it.

I have to admit that I am powerless over those feelings of incompetence and low self-worth. I have to learn that I can never make myself competent, and I can never make myself feel worthy. Once I realize that, I am truly powerless. But that's okay. God specializes in hopeless cases like mine. Others with similar problems have told me that God loves me regardless of what I can do or how I look. He loves me for me. God is giving me the faith to believe them and to believe him.

I choose to feel better about myself today, not because of someone else's words but because of God's.

Creator God, I believe you love me for who I am.

Step Two: Came to believe that a power greater than ourselves could restore us to sanity.

Scripture: Do you not know? Have you not heard? The Lord is the everlasting God, the Creator of the ends of the earth. He will not grow tired or weary, and his understanding no one can fathom. He gives strength to the weary and increases the power of the weak. Even youths grow tired and weary, and young men stumble and fall; but those who hope in the Lord will renew their strength. They will soar on wings like eagles; they will run and not grow weary, they will walk and not be faint. (Isa. 40:28–31)

The rumble of the jet engines and the hissing of the air began to get on my nerves. At least the flight would be over soon. Then I could say good-bye to this headache and the motor-mouthed stranger beside me. I thought of the few times my wife and I had made this trip across the country in our tiny car, sleeping in a two-person tent. Once we weathered a Nebraska tornado: We went to sleep in Nebraska and woke up in Iowa! We could have bought plane tickets with the money we spent on speeding tickets. I tried to save money and control the trip. It didn't work.

My attempts at "self-help" ended only in failure. My ways were as slow and painful as crossing the country in a tiny and crowded car. No room. No freedom. And we always arrived weary and worn. God's ways are different.

Trusting God instead of ourselves for recovery is much the same thing. God is able to lift us above our inability and powerlessness. Like the jet (or eagle) we effortlessly soar in his strength. Don't ask me how. I just believe.

Last time I traveled, there were tornados in Nebraska again. But I didn't care. I flew over them.

God, exchange my strength for yours.

Step Two: Came to believe that a power greater than ourselves could restore us to sanity.

Scripture: For I am convinced that neither death nor life, neither angels nor demons, neither height nor depth, nor anything else in all creation, will be able to separate us from the love of God that is in Christ Jesus our Lord. (Rom. 8:38–39)

The man being interviewed on television admitted that he was an alcoholic. Although he had been a sports hero years ago, he was a nobody, forgotten. In a solemn tone he told how he destroyed three marriages and lost his children. The interviewer noted a few trophies in the humble apartment, but the fallen hero continued talking about his disease. "I lost everything and everyone dear to me. I don't blame them. I drove them away."

The interviewer now acknowledged the man's need to discuss his life. He asked, "What changed you?"

"Not what. Who." For the first time this monster of a man began to wipe tears with his mighty hands. "He never left me. My insanity and disease couldn't drive him away."

"Who? A former teammate?" asked the interviewer.

"No. God. He waited. He loved me when no one else could or should have. When I didn't love myself." The focus of the interview went to film clips of the athlete in former days of glory, but I couldn't forget the gratitude I saw in this humbled man. God never left him.

What or who can separate me from God's love? Nothing and no one. Not even me.

Faithful God, I believe you love me even when I don't love myself.

***Step Two: Came to believe that a power greater than ourselves
could restore us to sanity.***

Scripture: *So do not fear, for I am with you; do not be dismayed, for
I am your God. I will strengthen you and help you; I will uphold you
with my righteous right hand. (Isa. 41:10)*

As a freshman in high school, I got
picked on a lot. It was mostly my fault. You see, I took typing
instead of "Ag" (Agriculture) during my first semester. In a farm
town that is nothing short of stupid if you're a boy. I was immediately labeled as a sissy. And I had the bruises to show it.

Things changed the following year. My little brother came
to high school. Rex, however, wasn't so little; he was born full
grown. Even the doctor who delivered him was intimidated. Rex
is a legend in my hometown. Anyone there can tell the story of
how Brent, the worst bully, approached Rex in his first football
practice. Brent grabbed a part of Rex's chest and said, "Whistle."
But before Brent had finished saying the word, Rex had cata-
pulted him across the locker room with one powerful blow. Brent
had a very colorful face for a week or two. And I was never
touched again.

Rex was my protector in high school, but I found that God is
even stronger than my brother. I have come to believe that God
is with me wherever I go. I can face every problem and bully
with his help. I can even face myself.

I don't care how the world may label me. In God, I know I'm
special and loved and protected.

O God my strength, be near me.

Step Two: Came to believe that a power greater than ourselves could restore us to sanity.

Scripture: For God so loved the world that he gave his only Son, that whoever believes in him shall not perish but have eternal life. For God did not send his Son into the world to condemn the world, but to save the world through him. (John 3:16–17)

John 3:16 is such a wonderful verse. It declares God's grace and love. But I can't help but feel that some believers fail to read the next verse: "For God did not send his Son into the world to condemn. . . ." I'm thinking of a young man who had a very troubled childhood.

It's easy to notice him in his mother's strict church (that is, if he goes). He gets up several times during the service, squirms when he is seated, and bolts out the door during the final prayer. As the preacher screams out condemnation against pornography, drunkenness, lust, and sin, the young man fumes because he knows that he is guilty as charged. And just below his anger lies his shame, and just below his shame lies his despair. Later, as he waits alone in the parking lot, he is anything but uplifted. He hates these people and their God.

Do you know who needs a doctor? The sick. Do you know who needs a redeemer? The lost and hurting. Do you know who Christ came for? This young man and others like him. Like me. Like you? God so loved that he sent help, not condemnation.

When I'm being judged, I squirm too. But when I'm being loved, I change.

God of love and grace, please save me.

STEP THREE

*Made a decision to turn
our will and our lives
over to the care of God
as we understood him.*

*T*herefore, I urge you, brothers,
in view of God's mercy, to offer
your bodies as living sacrifices,
holy and pleasing to God—which is
your spiritual worship. *(Rom. 12:1)*

Step Three Reflections

Step Three helps us remember a very important facet of God's nature: God will not force us into a decision that we're not willing to make. Although God's will may be the best for us, we are not always willing to accept that fact. We need time.

God told Noah about his plans to bring a great flood. Then God gave Noah 120 years to get used to the idea. God told Abraham about his desire to make a great nation from his seed. Then God waited most of Abraham's lifetime before the plan began to come true. God told Moses about his intention to free the Hebrew slaves in Egypt. Then God gave Moses forty years in the desert tending sheep to prepare. And God told the Virgin Mary of his purpose to bring a savior from her womb. Then God gave Mary thirty years of mothering before she saw the Messiah in her son.

All of these heroes of faith had to chose God's will daily. In the periods of waiting and preparation, they had to continually remember God's promise and plan, and they had to choose to trust. Nothing was forced upon them. They offered themselves to God as willing servants every day.

We have admitted our powerlessness, we have come to believe that God can restore us to sanity, and now, we must decide to turn our will and our lives over to God's care. We will not make this decision just once. We will make it every day, many times a day. Deciding to choose our will is a way of death. Deciding to choose God's will for us is a way of life.

Step Three: *Made a decision to turn our will and our lives over to the care of God as we understood him.*

Scripture: *Trust in the Lord with all your heart and lean not on your own understanding; in all your ways acknowledge him, and he will make your paths straight. (Prov. 3:5–6)*

I don't know if you have ever had to deal with pain in your joints, but I have. Once, the pain in my shoulder was so great that my orthopedic specialist suggested surgery as the only answer. It was to be my first surgery as an adult, but I reacted like a frightened child. I feared never waking up from anesthesia, waking up during surgery, having a crippled shoulder, and a host of other unreasonable possibilities. Unreasonable, that is, until I saw what I had to sign before the operation. Everything I signed seemed to say "Anything could go wrong! And it won't be the doctor's fault." I was ready to visit a medicine man I know in Arizona when the doctor himself came in the room.

I was very fond of my doctor, so I admitted my anxieties as he listened patiently. Finally he said, "If you die during surgery, I'll take out your next joint for free." We laughed until my fretting was just a memory. The next morning he performed the operation, and I didn't die or wake up during the surgery.

The pain made me seek the scalpel, but my trust allowed me to submit to it. Recovery works the same way. My pain caused me to see my powerlessness and need. My faith brought me to believe in God. And my trust in him frees me to turn my will and life over to his care.

Healer of my soul, I trust you with my life.

Step Three: Made a decision to turn our will and our lives over to the care of God as we understood him.

Scripture: Teach me to do your will, for you are my God; may your good Spirit lead me on level ground. (Ps. 143:10–11)

I went straight from the farm to Navy boot camp. I lost my clothes, hair, and identity all in one day. My new world was one of rules, regiment, and respect. I got up on Navy time, ate when I was told, washed my own clothes, made my own bed, marched until my feet throbbed, and did things that made no sense. Why did we carry the flag everywhere we marched? Or turn on a dime when the commander screamed? Why, for heaven's sake, did we have to get a whiff of tear gas?

Later, I learned the answers to a few of my questions. We were in enemy waters in Southeast Asia attempting to rescue American lives and property. Twenty marines had just died before our eyes, and our frigate was to tow a disabled ship to safety. As we pulled alongside this lost American ship, tear gas hovered above the deck. Our crew listened obediently for the captain's every command. Marines boarded the ship, and as their first act of liberation, they raised our flag. I've never been so proud.

In recovery, I've had to abandon my old ways and learn God's plan for me. When I gave God my will and life, he entered me into his boot camp, commanded by his Spirit. I was led and taught according to God's will, not mine. At first, I didn't understand his ways, but, today, I see his wisdom as I enjoy his peace.

God, Captain of the Hosts of Heaven, I give you my life. Lead on.

Step Three: Made a decision to turn our will and our lives over to the care of God as we understood him.

Scripture: Therefore, I urge you, brothers, in view of God's mercy, to offer your bodies as living sacrifices, holy and pleasing to God—which is your spiritual worship. (Rom. 12:1)

*D*uring college I studied ancient religions. I found the practice of human sacrifices most impressive and abhorrent. One ancient goddess named Molech required that babies be offered to her alive. The children passed into a great furnace shaped in the form of this cruel deity. The practice offended God. But more, God was enraged when his people participated. God wanted his people to know that he was not like the other gods. He desired only good for them, not destruction. Yet they chose to understand God through the distorted kaleidoscope of other religions. They should have trusted his word and his kind acts.

We act much the same way when it comes to trusting God with our lives. Instead of taking God at his word, we tend to view God through our own distortions. We think God looks like our parents, who may have been brutal. Or we think that God is as sickly as the churches we know. We may even think that God looks like us, a ball of fear and inability. But God is like God. He is not like my dad, my church, or myself. His word declares that he is kind and full of mercy. God is above our dysfunction.

God asks me to offer myself to him as a living sacrifice for my own good and not to appease some morbid desire in him. When I give myself to God, he gives me a new life in return.

God of mercy, I offer myself to you.

Step Three: Made a decision to turn our will and our lives over to the care of God as we understood him.

Scripture: Yet all who received him, to those who believed in his name, he gave the right to become children of God—children born not of natural descent, nor of human decision or a husband's will, but born of God. (John 1:12–13)

My sister and brother-in-law live on a farm. When their three girls were nearly grown and leaving for college, they began to think about the day when the nest would be empty. They asked me to help them adopt. Soon after, I met a young woman who was without a place to live. She was pregnant and not welcome in her parents' home. Her mom had told her that she could return only after a doctor had removed the problem. But she chose to carry the baby and asked me to help her adopt it out.

Well, eight years have now passed. And my nephew is a born farmer. He can tell you how to milk cows, cultivate corn, sow oats, and, of course, drive tractors. My nephew was a welcome addition to my sister's family. Not only is he loved and wanted, but he is also an heir to the farm.

God has welcomed us into his family in much the same way. We had an unsure future awaiting us. Pain and dysfunction marked our lives. But God opened his arms and his home to us and made us his own. And now, as we place our lives in his care, he teaches us about life in his kingdom, a kingdom where we are valued. Our futures now hold promise instead of pain.

Heavenly Father, thank you for adopting me.

Step Three: Made a decision to turn our will and our lives over to the care of God as we understood him.

Scripture: *"Come to me, all you who are weary and burdened, and I will give you rest. Take my yoke upon you and learn from me, for I am gentle and humble in heart, and you will find rest for your souls. For my yoke is easy and my burden is light." (Matt. 11:28–30)*

A lawyer once complained to me that working with hurting families was too burdensome for him. Issues of child custody and abuse caused him many sleepless nights when the faces of innocent children haunted him at night. He visualized them being passed around like property or forgotten in foster homes. One day he said, "I don't think I can do this much more. I'm going back to practicing tax law. I'd rather fight the IRS than face these children."

I encouraged him by explaining that he is God's warehouseman, not God's warehouse. I said, "It's not our job to hold life's burdens. We are only supposed to carry them to God. He alone can handle their load and bear their weight."

The wisdom that I shared with my friend was a direct result of practicing Step Three. When I turned my will and my life over to the care of God, I also gave him my burdens. I gave him the weight of my load, a load that I could never manage. God taught me how me how to be a warehouseman. I lift my burdens only long enough to carry them to God.

I saw my friend this week. I asked how the IRS was. He said, "I wouldn't know, I've been too busy carrying little ones to God."

Mighty God, I give you my burdens. Please give me your rest.

Step Three: Made a decision to turn our will and our lives over to the care of God as we understood him.

Scripture: *It is better to take refuge in the Lord than to trust in man. It is better to take refuge in the Lord than to trust in princes. (Ps. 118:8–9)*

*U*nless you are new to our planet, you have been hurt by others. You have been betrayed by friends and abused by those you loved. I had a close friend with whom I shared many confidences. Then one day, with little warning, he was gone. Only through the grapevine did I hear of his gossip. Nearly every confidential thing I had shared with him was now public knowledge. I was angry, I felt betrayed, and I wanted revenge.

For a very long time, I found it hard to disclose personal information about myself. In fact, I often sat mute in the Twelve-Step meetings I attended. Even though other members always said, "What's said here stays here," I didn't trust them. Then God got ahold of me. I realized that I couldn't control this man. I was powerless to manage my life or his. So I entrusted the whole mess to God.

With my trust came peace. I knew that God was different. I could trust him to hear of my life and not hurt me with the knowledge. God was the only one I confided in for a long time. I learned during that time that God could be a friend—closer than a brother. He knows all about me. He knows my sin, my weakness, my lust, my fears. Yet he still loves me. And he won't abandon me when I fail him.

Good friends are hard to find. God is not.

God, friends may fail, but your love is eternal.

Step Three: Made a decision to turn our will and our lives over to the care of God as we understood him.

Scripture: Going a little farther, he fell with his face to the ground and prayed, "My Father, if it is possible, may this cup be taken from me. Yet not as I will, but as you will." (Matt. 26:30)

I heard someone once say that he didn't dare give his life over to God. He just knew that if he gave himself to God, God would make him marry an ugly girl who couldn't kiss. I know what he means. Turning my life and will over to God means trusting him for the biggest decisions in my life: my job, my town, my future, my friends, my money, and more. He might make me wear out-of-date clothes or drive a car even older than what I've got. He might send me to do missionary work halfway around the world.

It is a struggle to turn our lives over to God's care. But that's okay. Even Jesus struggled with God's will. That's the thing I love about the story of Christ's prayer in the garden of Gethsemane. There was Jesus, the Son of God, and yet he struggled with his Father's will. He knew that God loved him and wanted his best, yet he struggled. That makes me feel better about my doubts and fears.

I know in my heart that God's will is best. But I also know that the decision to trust is not easy. And one more thing I know: I'm glad I'm already married.

Jesus, I know you understand my struggle. Thanks for being human too.

Step Three: Made a decision to turn our will and our lives over to the care of God as we understood him.

Scripture: I have been crucified with Christ and I no longer live, but Christ lives in me. The life I live in the body, I live by faith in the Son of God, who loved me and gave himself for me. (Gal. 2:20)

Since she was four or five years old, my daughter has been driving. She sits on my lap as we maneuver around a large empty lot. I put my foot on the gas, and she puts her foot on mine. I control the brake, but she steers. In almost every driving episode she will panic, cover her eyes, and plead for my intervention. It usually happens when we are headed for a wall without room to navigate. I put on the brake, back us up, and pull her hands away from her eyes. Then she starts all over.

Living life in recovery is a lot like my daughter's driving. After I admitted my powerlessness and came to believe in God's concern for me, I invited him to take control of my life. I am still living my life now, but I'm not really driving the car. If you look very closely at the controls, you'll see that Christ has his foot on the gas and the brake. He's actually the one in control, and I'm enjoying life for a change. Although I pretend to be in control now and then, I don't really want to drive.

Before I decided to trust Christ, I had nothing but one wreck after another. But under his guidance, I feel safe. The other day, I faced a problem that, in former days, would have sent me into panic. But this time I didn't seek a way to kill the pain, I gave God the problem. And he kept me from hitting the wall.

God, I'm content to leave the driving to you. Keep me safe.

Step Three: *Made a decision to turn our will and our lives over to the care of God as we understood him.*

Scripture: *Commit to the Lord whatever you do, and your plans will succeed. (Prov. 16:3)*

*J*ake was eighteen. He had just enough money, but he got butterflies every time he thought about buying it. His sweaty hand guarded the cache of bills bulging in his pocket. Without anyone's knowledge he headed for Crazy Carl's Used Cars to buy the car of his dreams. His family was shocked when he drove home—especially Dad who stood silent.

The car had a Crazy Carl's fourteen-day unconditional guarantee. By day fifteen, the transmission was slipping. By day eighteen, the transmission was gone. The mechanic at Crazy Carl's said it was a five-hundred-dollar repair, almost half of what Jake paid for the car. A humbled Jake now asked, "What should I do, Dad?" Without any judging or criticizing, Jake's dad laid out the logical options and suggested the one he felt was best. He also offered help.

As Jake was afraid to commit his car-buying plan to his father, I am sometimes afraid to commit my plans to the Lord. He might tell me no. Or God might tell me to wait. He might even make me chose a different way. But also, as Jake failed, I have blown it enough to know that God's ways really are best for me.

Nevertheless, if I get stubborn, you'll probably see me along the freeway with a blown transmission. Promise you'll wave.

Heavenly Father, forgive my stubbornness and fear.

Step Three: Made a decision to turn our will and our lives over to the care of God as we understood him.

Scripture: I tell you the truth, anyone who has faith in me will do what I have been doing. He will do even greater things than these, because I am going to the Father. And I will do whatever you ask in my name, so that the Son may bring glory to the Father. (John 14:12–13)

While I served as a chaplain for the Los Angeles Sheriff's department, I came into contact with many peace officers. Every cop has a different and personal reason for choosing a career in law enforcement. Those reasons can be self-serving or they can be altruistic. But the worst reason of all is the need for power. These cops are cops only because of the badge and gun. The words service and community have no meaning for them.

I think of these guys when I read the above verse. For years, I've heard Christians quote it as proof that Jesus wants his disciples to do great miracles and amazing feats. But Jesus said, ". . . anyone who has faith in me will do what I have been doing." And what was he doing? He was sharing and showing the good news that God reigns, God forgives, God sets free, and God meets his people's needs. Jesus performed miracles to serve people, not to show people how powerful he was.

The kingdom of God was evident in Jesus' life for one reason: He was obedient to God's will. I want to do as Jesus did, but it begins with making the decision to turn my life and will over to God's rule, not mine. If I get my badge and gun in God's kingdom, it will be to do his will, not mine.

King above, thy will be done in my life as it is in heaven.

Step Three: *Made a decision to turn our will and our lives over to the care of God as we understood him.*

Scripture: *"For I know the plans I have for you," declares the Lord, "plans to prosper you and not to harm you, plans to give you hope and a future. Then you will call upon me and come and pray to me, and I will listen to you. You will seek me and find me when you seek me with all your heart. I will be found by you," declares the Lord. (Jer. 29:11–14)*

"**J**oin the Navy and see the world." I did. I was captivated by the many temples, shrines, icons, and idols throughout Asia. I saw gods shaped in the images of poisonous snakes, monkeys, cats, and multi-faced beasts. In Hong Kong, I saw the gold-plated corpse of an old man. In every case, worshipers worked hard to keep the gods happy.

If you shaped God from your image of him, what would he look like? Many of us have gods who look like abusive parents. We see God as condemning, disapproving, unforgiving, and never happy with us. It's hard to imagine a good and loving God.

Do you know what God really looks like? I can tell you exactly. He looks like Jesus. Jesus said, "If you've seen me, you've seen the Father." When we look at Jesus' life, we see that he spent his time with the sinners, the outcasts, the downtrodden, the rejected. He taught of forgiveness, healing, mercy, and grace. Jesus taught that God is approachable. Sinners are to be drawn near. Jesus clearly demonstrated through his words, actions, and sacrifice that God's plan for us is good and redemptive.

I'm glad that when God showed himself to us, he did it with the warmth and love of Christ.

God of grace, I know your plan for me is good.

STEP FOUR

Made a searching and fearless moral inventory of ourselves.

*L*et us examine our ways and test them, and let us return to the Lord. *(Lam. 3:40)*

Step Four Reflections

When we work Step Four, it is good to remember this important fact: God completely knows our individual nature. He knows our sins, he knows our failings, he knows our weaknesses, he knows our hearts. And he knows one more thing—that we can't see ourselves without his help. So again in partnership with God, we begin to look inward.

God has walked this way many times with many great biblical figures. God helped the wicked citizens of Nineveh see their faults and failings. He searched King David's heart and sent the prophet Nathan to uncover David's sin. He used prophets to bring the nation of Israel to a place of self-understanding. And God used the crowing of a simple rooster to point out the Apostle Peter's failure. The point: We don't begin or finish this moral inventory on our own. God goes with us every step of the way. He uncovers the defects and flaws so that we can see them and grow beyond their influence. Then he carries the weight of our sins and defects so that we will not be forever burdened and broken by their strain.

But God helps us see more than just our failings. He also helps us see our strengths. Throughout the pages of the Bible, God has chosen ordinary people for his work. And in almost every case, God pointed out to these seemingly ordinary people the fact that they possessed unique strengths and abilities. He told a seventeen-year-old prophet named Jeremiah that he had the courage to face a sinful nation with the truth of their failures. God told an insecure soldier named Joshua that he had the ability to lead a nation into the promised land. God told a hot-tempered fisherman named Peter that he was a rock and a foundation for the new Church. And God points out our strengths and talents today. He wants us to know them and become comfortable with them.

This part of our journey promises tears and embarrassment as well as insights and encouragement. Look forward to Step Four, for in it, we see ourselves with God's help. This step must not frighten us. Remember, all those near to us, especially God, have seen our failings and flaws for years. It's time *we* see ourselves.

Step Four: Made a searching and fearless moral inventory of ourselves.

Scripture: *The heart is deceitful above all things and beyond cure. Who can understand it? I the Lord search the heart and examine the mind, to reward a man according to his conduct, according to what his deeds deserve. (Jer. 17:9–10)*

Another parishioner had just called and wanted to know something about my weekend. Just last Sunday I had announced my plan to take a rare weekend off. We couldn't afford to go anywhere special, so we just intended to relax at home. But the phone kept ringing. And because of my inability, as a codependent, to establish good barriers, I had just "bent the truth" for this last caller. I had told her that we were leaving town; I hoped that would keep her from calling again. But my wife heard every word.

After I had hung up the phone, my wife said, "Doesn't the Holy Spirit ever convict you of lying?" I didn't see it that way. I saw it as protection. But my wife's comment sent me into a depression. And my depression drove me to prayer. In my prayer time, God showed me how my lying was really a sinful escape, a form of manipulation, and a serious character flaw. God also showed me how my inability to establish barriers was a source of constant vulnerability, an invitation for failure. My depression didn't improve. Seeing my sinful heart wasn't pretty, but I felt a strange peace even in the depression. Just owning up to my failures opened a door for serenity.

The first moral defect on my Step Four inventory wasn't "bending the truth," it was *lying*.

Righteous God, show me my deceitful heart but not all at once.

***Step Four:** Made a searching and fearless moral inventory of ourselves.*

Scripture: *While Peter was below in the courtyard, one of the servant girls. . . . saw Peter warming himself. . . . "You also were with . . . Jesus," she said. But he denied it. . . . and went out into the entryway. When the servant girl saw him there, she said again to those standing around, "This fellow is one of them." . . . He began to call down curses on himself, and swore. . . . Immediately the rooster crowed . . . and he broke down and wept. (Mark 14:66–72)*

*F*ive-year-old R.J. woke up in pain and looked like a chipmunk. We thought it was mumps, but the doctor said strep throat. The antibiotics started working fast, but his glands remained sore. The next day, R.J. was hard at play. The boys invaded our house forty-'leven times. They looted the fridge and made off with soda, juice, and cookies. Each invasion grew louder, and I grew angrier. I was trying to get some important work done on the computer.

Finally I lost it. I screamed, "Out!" No one heard me. In desperation, I moved straight toward R.J. and grabbed the back of his neck and roared. But R.J. began to cry, "Dad, that's where I hurt." The other boys ran for cover, and R.J. fled to his room.

R.J. was still crying when I entered his room. I felt like a monster. As I sat beside my precious boy and looked into his eyes, all I could do was cry. I forgot the reason for my anger. I just saw my sin—my selfishness and my rage—I saw it in R.J.'s eyes, in R.J.'s pain.

I left R.J. to compose myself, but he followed. He put his little hand on my knee and said, "Is that the first time you cried since you were a parent?"

Step Four brings tears as it brings a picture of our real selves, of our failures.

God, help me see the signals that point to my sin even when they point with tiny hands.

Step Four: Made a searching and fearless moral inventory of ourselves.

Scripture: *If anyone thinks he is something when he is nothing, he deceives himself. Each one should test his own actions. Then he can take pride in himself, without comparing himself to somebody else, for each one should carry his own load. (Gal. 6:3–5)*

*I*f you wanted to know how to do anything, all you had to do was ask Jim. He was the church's resident know-it-all. He would tell you the best medicine to help your arthritis or the best fertilizer for your roses. He might tell you how to fix your car or heal your marriage. He was an expert in child discipline and a self-declared Bible scholar. He even had an eye for fashion. At any time he might invade private conversations with something to add, even if the discussion was "girl talk."

Jim's posturing didn't reflect the reality of his life, and everyone knew it. In reality, Jim wasn't very successful. His wife had left him for another man. His children didn't want to live with him. He was unemployed. His car was always in need of repair. And at night, he laid his lonely head on the sofa at a friend's place. If Jim had not been so personally offensive, I suppose the folks might have felt sorry for him. But they didn't. They avoided him.

Many of us are like Jim—we never seem to get it. We never see ourselves. Pains, problems, or poverty can't convince us of the need to examine ourselves. That's where Step Four helps. Step Four makes self-examination a priority. It turns our focus inward to see the good and the not-so-good.

God, help me to stop fixing others and to start examining myself.

Step Four: Made a searching and fearless moral inventory of ourselves.

Scripture: Let us examine our ways and test them, and let us return to the Lord. (Lam. 3:40)

*D*uring Step Four, I had no trouble dredging up all the defects in my life and character. My trouble began when I started to take an inventory of my positive traits. I was stumped. When I did think of something positive, I felt guilty.

One day, I scratched out a list of what I wished I was. I did it really fast before the committee in my head could protest. And when I reviewed the list, I could see myself there. I really do love people. I really am a good speaker. I really do have a sense of humor. I am a competent leader. I am a faithful husband and devoted father. But before I could make it halfway down my wish list, the committee had convened in my head. "Wait a minute!" the chairman gruffed. "Who said you love people? You hate people. Plus, you sound stupid when you speak. You have no sense of humor. You're depressed all the time. If you're such a good leader, how come you're burned out? You ignore your wife and kids. You're just a loser."

I kept my list over the protest of the committee in my head. I kept it because a man in a Twelve-Step meeting shared an experience just like mine. The same committee lived in his head. But he learned to accept his positive traits by faith. God told him that he had value and that he had God-given gifts that needed to be recognized and used.

Help me, God, to see myself through your eyes.

Step Four: Made a searching and fearless moral inventory of ourselves.

Scripture: Search me, O God, and know my heart; test me and know my anxious thoughts. See if there is any offensive way in me, and lead me in the way everlasting. (Ps. 139:23–24)

*T*he Lord came to Sam one night in his dreams. Christ stood beside the bed with flashlight in hand. He motioned for Sam to follow. Sam got up but asked, "Where are we going, Lord?"

"We are going into the cellar of your heart, son. There is something down there that must come out," the Lord answered. When the pair reached the bottom of the stairs, the Lord extended the flashlight and illuminated a large bush. "This one must come out. You've had it for too long." Sam pulled and tugged with the Lord's help until the thorny and vile bush came out. The Lord then led the way up the stairs and back to bed.

Now in bed, Sam felt so much better. He felt lighter, as if an awful load had been removed. One thing, however, haunted Sam. When the Lord had illuminated the one bush for him, Sam saw the shadows of many other bushes in the background. But that was okay. Sam knew that he would deal with the others in God's time. And he also knew that he wouldn't have to go down there alone.

Taking a searching and fearless moral inventory is a very serious and painful task. But in the Twelve-Step program, it is never undertaken alone. God will always be our guide—a guide who points out our defects (or bushes) for our good and for our transformation.

Searching Lord, here is my hand; take me to the cellar and show me myself.

Step Four: *Made a searching and fearless moral inventory of ourselves.*

Scripture: *My dear brothers, take note of this: Everyone should be quick to listen, slow to speak and slow to become angry, for man's anger does not bring about the righteous life that God desires. Therefore, get rid of all moral filth and the evil that is so prevalent, and humbly accept the word planted in you, which can save you. (James 1:19–21)*

*H*ave you ever heard about dogs who can forewarn an epileptic about a coming seizure? It's a gift, not a learned behavior. In a similar vein, I have noticed that my dog, Good Girl, can warn me about my anger. I have always had to watch my tendency to control others with volume and fury. But Good Girl can sense my mood and temper before I've even spoken a word. It is an amazing gift for which I am very thankful.

A few years ago, I allowed pressures from church to affect my whole life. I was filled with anger. I couldn't show it at church, and I hadn't given it to God. So I often brought it home. As I walked in the door each night, there she was waiting and wagging her tail. If I was angry, Good Girl would lay her ears back and very cautiously lick my hand. I could see my sin in her timid approach. So before I could offend or hurt, I would head back out the door and walk around the park until I had poured out my anger to God. He was the only one able to hear me fume without being hurt or offended.

My abusive anger was a serious defect. Although God alone was able to hear and heal it, everyone felt it—especially my friend.

God, you see my anger. Help me see it too.

Step Four: *Made a searching and fearless moral inventory of ourselves.*

Scripture: *There is no fear in love. But perfect love drives out fear, because fear has to do with punishment. The man who fears is not made perfect in love.* (1 John 4:18)

*K*evin knew he shouldn't be playing with Dad's tools, but he wanted to build a birdhouse. Kevin figured that if he did the job in the yard, his dad wouldn't find a mess on his workbench. He finished in plenty of time and put all the tools back—he thought.

The following week Kevin's older brother hit something while mowing the lawn. He hit Dad's expensive side-cutters. And now they were rusted and nicked. "Boy, are you gonna get it when Dad sees these!" Kevin's brother taunted. "You know his tools are off limits, you dummy!"

Kevin knew his brother would tell. So he waited in his room for his dad, who soon entered with tool in hand. As he sat beside Kevin he asked for the story. Kevin obliged. The dad told his son how much a new tool would cost and how he expected him to replace it. Kevin understood.

Although the boy was sober and respectful throughout the encounter, he was never afraid. This had happened many times over various blunders. And Kevin knew two important things about his dad. He was fair, and he loved Kevin, very much.

We needn't ever be afraid of exposing our defects before our heavenly Father. He too is fair, and he loves us, very much.

Heavenly Father, my list of blunders is more than I can bear. Thanks for still loving me.

Step Four: *Made a searching and fearless moral inventory of ourselves.*

Scripture: Examine yourselves to see whether you are in the faith; test yourselves. Do you not realize that Christ Jesus is in you—unless, of course, you fail the test? And I trust that you will discover that we have not failed the test. (2 Cor. 13:5–6)

*N*ot long ago we had a rather intense earthquake. The early morning tremor brought our local newscasters scrambling to cover the story. On one station, a well-known anchorman had his hairpiece on crooked. On another station, a reporter had caught a part of his shirttail in his zipper. In each case the men were trying to dispense a serious and important message, but their appearance kept us laughing. I couldn't help but wonder if either men had looked in a mirror or examined himself before he stepped in front of the camera.

Paul reminds us in 2 Corinthians 13:5–6 that it is our responsibility to test ourselves. Examining ourselves as Christians really isn't a difficult task. Are we in the faith? And is Christ in us? It comes down to one simple and very practical word: trust. Do we trust our recovery to God or ourselves? Do we trust God or ourselves for our daily bread and shelter? Do we trust God or ourselves for our righteousness? Do we trust God or ourselves for eternal life?

Maybe a cockeyed hairpiece or messed-up zipper won't tell you about your trust. But the anxious knot in your stomach will. The testy demeanor will. The late-night sleeplessness and worry will. If you fail the test, don't worry. Just add "doubt" to your inventory like I do.

Great Provider, I trust you with my recovery, my family, my health, my sustenance, my soul.

Step Four: *Made a searching and fearless moral inventory of ourselves.*

Scripture: *Get rid of all bitterness, rage and anger, brawling and slander, along with every form of malice. (Eph. 4:31)*

She waited for the others to leave so that she could be alone with the casket. The others cried and held one another as they left, but she stood rigid and quiet. He was so still now. His lips forever sealed. His hands forever folded. His eyes forever shut. And now she was finally free—she hoped.

A tear finally found its way down her cheek. But it wasn't for him. With fists clenched and jaws tightened she leaned forward and spoke in his ear. She spoke low but with force, "You will never hurt me again!"

For many years she wanted to be rid of the hatred and bitterness she felt for her dad. But now, even his death didn't seem to finish her intense torment, a suffering that kept her from life. Being close to any man caused her pain, but she so wanted a family. She wanted love.

As a result of her involvement with a Twelve-Step group, she accomplished Step Four. Among her moral defects she felt compelled to list bitterness and anger. It was then that she realized that those emotions were her responsibility. She had to own them and not blame them away in denial. She couldn't change the pain he caused her yesterday, but she could change the pain today. And with God's help she has.

God of Power and Grace, I see my bitterness and rage, and I don't want it anymore.

Step Four: Made a searching and fearless moral inventory of ourselves.

Scripture: I remember my affliction and my wandering, the bitterness and the gall. I well remember them, and my soul is downcast within me. Yet this I call to mind and therefore I have hope: Because of the Lord's great love we are not consumed, for his compassions never fail. (Lam. 3:19–22)

*I*t took me four painful months to work Step Four. When I finished with my inventory, I gazed upon a list much longer than I could have ever imagined. As I looked closely and saw all my moral failings and sins, I wondered how anyone could love or want me. How could I be a father or husband or friend? My list seemed to reinforce all my feelings of worthlessness. I've got to be honest, I was depressed for some time.

The thing that brought a change in me was a memory. I remembered Brian G., my only sponsor. Brian, an alcoholic, opened the Twelve Steps up for me. But he was gone now. Moved. Yet I had memories. I had heard his story many times, and I was always amazed that he found the courage to go on after all his losses—self-inflicted losses. Estranged wives, family, friends, and employers litter his past, and he was to blame. "How can you handle the guilt and pain of knowing your failures?" I asked.

Brian simply answered, "I don't handle it. If I tried, I'd be drunk right now. I face my sin. God handles it. Others may not forgive me, and I may not forgive myself. But this I know—God accepts me, warts and all."

Brian was somewhere in Arizona when I needed him. But that's okay. I remembered his example. I remembered his God.

God, my past is more than I can bear. Please handle it.

Step Four: *Made a searching and fearless moral inventory of ourselves.*

Scripture: *Blessed is the man who perseveres under trial, because when he has stood the test, he will receive the crown of life that God has promised to those who love him. (James 1:12)*

I'm blessed to have a number of fine brothers-in-law. One in particular has persevered under great trial. He faithfully attended to the needs of his infirm parents until their deaths. He currently oversees care for his older sister, who entered a convalescent hospital after she lost her husband and her mental health. He provides support and counsel for his emotionally unstable younger sister who lives in an adult care facility. And finally, he is a dedicated husband and father, providing for my sister and their three children.

Just as my brother-in-law has persevered under trial, even so must we who are in recovery. We may not have family to care for, but we have ourselves. In a very real sense we are two people in one body. We have an infirm half and a responsible half. Our infirm side has to admit our powerlessness to care for ourselves; and our responsible half has to exercise faith in God to restore us to sanity. Our infirm part has to make the decision to turn our lives and wills over to God's care; and our responsible side must continue to persevere by taking an inventory of our defects and sins.

Caring for the infirm is not easy, but the rewards are great: serenity and peace with God, ourselves, and others.

God, I know that the way is not easy and the road is long. Give me strength to endure and succeed.

Step Four: Made a searching and fearless moral inventory of ourselves.

Scripture: Put to death, therefore, whatever belongs to your earthly nature: sexual immorality, impurity, lust, evil desires and greed, which is idolatry. Because of these, the wrath of God is coming. You used to walk in these ways, in the life you once lived. But now you must rid yourselves of all such things as these: anger, rage, malice, slander, and filthy language from your lips. (Col. 3:5–8)

*T*he girls quietly talked as Clyde stumbled in and settled himself at the bar. When he turned to get friendly, Janice recognized him; he was a coworker's husband. Janice fumed as she thought of his wife and children at home. But more, her anger was fueled by the bitterness she still felt for her estranged husband who had similar habits. She wanted to hurt Clyde or least make him go home. So she blurted out, "Hey Clyde, I just saw your wife, Sara. She won $500 at bingo tonight." It worked. He left. But it wasn't Clyde she hurt.

The next day Sara came to work with a bruised face. She told everyone it was a car accident, but Janice knew differently. When Clyde came home asking for the money, Sara had none. And Sara was punished for Janice's need to get even—to hurt.

No amount of apologizing ever made Janice feel forgiven. She knew what it was like to live with a cruel and abusive husband. And she relived her pain through Sara's torment. Janice's old ways had to go. Her anger and need for revenge only brought more pain.

The methods and means we have used to survive have no place in God's plan for us. God's ways are healing, not hurting.

Just Lord, I leave judgment and vengeance in your hands.
My anger will never accomplish your will.

STEP FIVE

---

*Admitted to God, to
ourselves, and to another
human being the exact
nature of our wrongs.*

*T*herefore confess your sins
to each other and pray for each
other so that you may be healed.
(James 5:16a)

Step Five Reflections

*O*ur success in Step Five is greatly enhanced when we keep in mind a very important part of God's nature: God, who knows our sin, wants us to confess it out loud and thereby bear witness to its existence. God, who knows all our needs before we ask, still wants us to ask. Although God knows all things, he still wants to hear our concerns, sins, and needs from us.

God also wants us to confess our faults to another human being. From the early days of the Law until the New Testament instructions, God has directed his people to confess their wrongs. In the early days of the Law, men would place their hands upon the scapegoat and confess their sins before the priests. In the days of the New Testament Church, believers were instructed to confess their sins to one another for forgiveness and healing. Admission of our wrongs to God, ourselves, and others opens a door to the innermost closet of our being. And the opening provides an opportunity for God to heal and change us. If the door is left unopened, the decay and poison of our own sin and moral defects will destroy our lives.

We have seen our sins, flaws, and defects in Step Four. Now, in Step Five, it is time to be honest about what we've found. We can start by telling God. He already knows what we'll say, but for our sakes, he wants to hear us tell him.

Next, we admit to ourselves. This may seem unnecessary, even foolish, but it's not. Denial has been a powerful force in many of our lives, keeping us blinded to the very actions, addictions, and attitudes which controlled our lives and stole our peace of mind. We must tell ourselves in Step Five that we recognize the wrongs which have impoverished our souls and imprisoned our serenity.

Finally, Step Five directs us to share the exact nature of our wrongs with another human being. This action requires courage because of our fear of rejection and disapproval, but if we trust the program's wisdom here, this act of confession promises new release and healing. In telling another living breathing soul, we release the power of hidden sin and we remove the power of self-condemnation.

Step Five: Admitted to God, to ourselves, and to another human being the exact nature of our wrongs.

Scripture: *Submit yourselves, then, to God. Resist the devil, and he will flee from you. Come near to God and he will come near you. Wash your hands, you sinners, and purify your hearts, you double-minded. (James 4:7–8)*

When Jesus appeared on the scene, he chastised the religious establishment for not properly receiving him. He said that they were like children in the marketplace who made fun of real life. When John the Baptist came sorrowfully in repentance, they wanted to play wedding. And when Jesus came, calling himself the bridegroom and celebrating the kingdom, they wanted to play funeral. His point was this: The response of the "religious types" did not match the hour. They needed to respond properly. The Messiah was in their midst, and they wanted to play with someone else. God is still looking for an appropriate response from his people.

After we work Step Four and see our defects, only one thing is called for. The only sane response is to seek help from the only one who can provide it. We must draw near God in repentance and confess our wrongs.

Whenever God does a work of grace in our lives, he stands back and allows us to respond. Showing us our defects and sins is a powerful work of grace. Now it is time to respond. We must not mock reality but face it. Don't play games with God.

Holy God, I see my sin, and now I choose to confess it.

Step Five: *Admitted to God, to ourselves, and to another human being the exact nature of our wrongs.*

Scripture: *O Lord, we acknowledge our wickedness and the guilt of our fathers; we have indeed sinned against you. (Jer. 14:20)*

One day I was discussing taxes with a close friend of mine, who is a recovering workaholic and codependent. He was boasting about his excessively high tax bill the year before. I figured he must be doing well in his business to pay that much in taxes. But later that day my friend called me and asked me to meet him. Over cheeseburgers he confessed to lying. "I didn't really pay that much in taxes. I exaggerated to impress you. I'm sorry."

I told my friend that he really didn't need to apologize to me for exaggerating. "After all," I said, wanting to break my uncomfortable tension, "I'm a preacher. I took Exaggeration 101 in seminary."

But my friend didn't laugh. Instead, he said, "One of my biggest defects is lying to impress others, and God won't let me get away with it anymore. I had to face it or lose the serenity and close fellowship that God is sharing with me. And I value God's closeness more than your admiration."

Once the Lord helps us identify a moral defect or flaw, we are responsible for our knowledge. Examining ourselves and confessing our faults keeps us in closer fellowship with the Lord and in closer contact with ourselves.

God, help me acknowledge my defects and sins. I'm tired of hiding them.

Step Five: Admitted to God, to ourselves, and to another human being the exact nature of our wrongs.

Scripture: So then, each of us will give an account of himself to God. (Rom. 14:12)

*T*he questionnaire asked the most personal questions about sex, perversion, drugs, alcohol, friends, weapons, childhood, and so on. But I figured becoming a reserve deputy sheriff was serious. Soon background investigators began to call us out one by one. I wanted any investigator but one. She was beautiful and very innocent looking, not at all the sort of person I wanted reviewing my past. But guess who picked up my file? Pamela.

I soon found that the questionnaire was for a lie-detector test, and it was Pamela's job to review it first. I had admitted to things in that questionnaire that no one on earth knows about me. But now Pamela knew. She also knew I was a pastor. As she reviewed the pages she kept looking up at me with her glasses perched on the tip of her nose. I just knew what she was thinking. "Yuk!" But somehow she didn't treat me like that.

The reason Step Five is so difficult is that we must confess the most intimate details of our lives to another. If we were telling just the good, it would be easy; but Step Five focuses on our wrongs. So we worry about what the other person will think, and we are tempted to tone down our list. But honesty and vulnerability is called for, that is, if we want healing.

Here's my list, Lord. This is what I'm really like. Help me find courage to tell another.

Step Five: Admitted to God, to ourselves, and to another human being the exact nature of our wrongs.

Scripture: *If we claim to be without sin, we deceive ourselves and the truth is not in us. If we confess our sins, he is faithful and just and will forgive us our sins and purify us from all unrighteousness. (1 John 1:8–9)*

"*I*'ve been really depressed and angry for the last couple of days and I don't know why," Eileen said to her sister Jane.

"Well, I never get down," Jane replied. "I don't allow it. I just read a particular Bible verse over and over until any hint of ill wind passes."

Eileen's coffee was getting cold but her temper wasn't. She countered, "Well, Jane, when you cover up your problems with repetitive Bible verses instead of facing them, that's called denial!" Eileen expected an angry comeback, but instead, she saw a tear form in her sister's eye. "I'm sorry. I didn't mean to . . ."

Jane responded with her eyes fixed on the coffee cup. "It's okay. You're not very tactful, but you're right. I'm human too. It's not that I don't allow bad feelings. It's just that I'm afraid to feel anything for fear of really losing it. People are being laid off at Jim's shop, the kids' problems overwhelm me, and I just don't feel healthy." Eileen moved to comfort and found two weak and trembling hands reaching out.

Our Christian faith is not a pass to exempt us from human frailties, emotions, or sins. It is our source of strength, encouragement, and hope in our weakness. Christians are sinners too. Confessing our sin keeps us honest.

Lord, give me a kindred spirit with whom I can share my sins, frailties, and needs.

Step Five: *Admitted to God, to ourselves, and to another human being the exact nature of our wrongs.*

Scripture: *When he came to his senses, he said, "How many of my father's hired men have food to spare, and here I am staving to death! I will set out and go back to my father and say to him: Father, I have sinned against heaven and against you. I am no longer worthy to be called your son; make me like one of your hired men." (Luke 15:17-19)*

Some years ago, I worked on a large church staff. In typical codependent style, I wore many hats and then grew bitter at the senior pastor who allowed me to do so much. In time, the church's malcontents found I had a willing ear for their concerns. I sympathized with their criticisms about the pastor. He wasn't community minded enough. He had his priorities askew. He didn't preach effectively. And he was a hermit. I now participated in the very thing that had so hurt my ministry just a year before.

Then one day, the pastor called me into his office. I went in with knocking knees and trembling voice. But I found that he wanted to discuss an upcoming special event for which I was responsible. As I sat in his office, time stood still. I beheld this wonderful man and felt so guilty. He had shown me nothing but benevolence, and I was repaying him with backbiting. He offered me support, and I returned subversion. What a fool I'd been.

When I emerged from my reverie, I interrupted the pastor. "I have something to share," I began. And for the next several minutes I confessed, cried, and ultimately found comfort. The pastor heard my confession, and like God, he forgave.

Heavenly Father, in our sinful way we have bitten the hand that feeds us. Have mercy upon us.

Step Five: *Admitted to God, to ourselves, and to another human being the exact nature of our wrongs.*

Scripture: When I kept silent, my bones wasted away through my groaning all day long. For day and night your hand was heavy upon me; my strength was sapped as in the heat of summer. . . . Then I acknowledged my sin to you and did not cover up my iniquity. I said, "I will confess my transgressions to the Lord"—and you forgave the guilt of my sin. . . . (Ps. 32:3–5)

I once asked a friend why he spoke so little of his parents. He explained that growing up in his mother's home was nothing to cherish. I pressed him, and he shared an incredible story about a mother who had insanely kept every single piece of trash, even the most vile, for over twenty years. He described a house bursting with clutter and garbage. And he recounted that when he was thirteen, his mother forced him from the home. Why? Because he tried to clean his room.

Following his mother's suicide, my friend showed me the home. Once inside the door, we ascended a mountain of trash and walked in a constant stoop with only a few feet of clearance from the ceiling. As we crawled through the living room, I was told that a piano could be found below. The house was beyond belief and took many weeks to clean.

This story is true, and it is not unlike our lives. Many of us have allowed sins, habits, resentments, failings, and many other vile things to accumulate in our lives. Our spirits are full of deadly poison. Step Four helped us identify the moral defects, and now Step Five will help us be rid of their stench. Step Five allows the doors to be opened and the sins to be aired.

God, my spirit is full of refuse and sin, but I chose to open the doors and stop concealing.

Step Five: Admitted to God, to ourselves, and to another human being the exact nature of our wrongs.

Scripture: Therefore confess your sins to each other and pray for each other so that you may be healed. The prayer of a righteous man is powerful and effective. (James 5:16)

I had a kindred spirit during my Navy days. Buddy was closer than a brother to me. Nothing was ever hidden between us. We found that as Christians our closeness provided the perfect opportunity for mutual confession. I often disclosed my deepest failings, and he transparently did the same.

One particular weakness constantly tormented Buddy, and he frequently upbraided himself for it. He had a very abusive, alcoholic father, and during his childhood, he tried many things to console himself. The one thing that brought him the most comfort was masturbation. For him it wasn't just sexual exploration, it was escape. It was a way to run from the pain and the abuse. But now he was thousands of miles from home and free to live life as he would. Yet he was still chained to this habit, and he often relied upon it for comfort and escape.

Buddy often confessed the weakness to me, and in time, he reported a growing change. He began to sense a different sort of comfort and escape just in his admission. My understanding brought the comfort, and his confession allowed the escape— escape from the power of hidden sin.

Confession does more than ease our conscience. It opens the door for the healing and change.

God of forgiveness and change, hear my sin and change my heart.

Step Five: Admitted to God, to ourselves, and to another human being the exact nature of our wrongs.

Scripture: He who conceals his sins does not prosper, but whoever confesses and renounces them finds mercy. (Prov. 28:13)

*D*aylight revealed a miniature mountain range of snowdrifts. My brother and I conquered every one. Atop the biggest drift, Rex began to dream about Mrs. Stevenson's candy dish. Mrs. Stevenson always allowed us to choose freely from the dish. We could see her house, but she was gone. That, however, didn't stop Rex. He proposed that we let ourselves in since she never locked her side door. I disagreed and left.

Later that day, the phone rang. It was Mrs. Stevenson. She wondered if we had seen anything strange around her house. She found her door ajar and melted snow on the rug. Wet footprints led to the candy dish.

Dad asked if we had visited Mrs. Stevenson's. I said, "No." And Rex said that he hadn't even been near her place for days. Dad seemed satisfied, but Mom looked probingly at Rex and hid something behind her back. The silence was thick.

"I did it, Mom," Rex burst out.

"I know you did," she answered, "but thanks for admitting it." She bent over to give him a hug, and I saw behind her back. She had a knit mitten with a piece of candy stuck on it.

We can't get away with anything before God. He knows even more than Mom does. And when we freely confess, his mercy never fails.

Heavenly Father, I won't hide anything from you. Please don't hide your mercy from me.

Step Five: Admitted to God, to ourselves, and to another human being the exact nature of our wrongs.

Scripture: If you have played the fool and exalted yourself, or if you have planned evil, clap your hand over your mouth! (Prov. 30:32)

I knew everybody in the meeting except one. He sat quietly at first, but after about six of us had shared some personal struggle or need, he spoke. He began to give each one of us advice. He had a cure for every problem. I started to get angry, not just at him, but I was angry at the leader who didn't stop this guy. "Advice isn't allowed!" I screamed inside my head. But just as quickly as he began, he stopped.

A number of others then shared, and we continued with our meeting. I kept one eye on this new guy and noticed a change in his countenance. Whereas before he had been on the edge of his seat and talkative, now he sat with hands folded and head down.

When the leader concluded and asked for prayer requests, this guy lifted his hand. He said, "Before you pray, I'd like to confess something." The leader nodded. "I'm sure that I have more problems than all of you combined, and I realize that it's not my job to fix you. If I keep fixing other people's lives, I'll never get around to mine." We ended with a special prayer just for him.

Once we actually confess our sins and faults out loud, it's easier to rise above them. Step Five can't prevent us from making old mistakes, but it can keep the old habits in plain view where we can keep an eye on them.

God, my old ways have caused me trouble enough. Help me to break old patterns.

Step Five: Admitted to God, to ourselves, and to another human being the exact nature of our wrongs.

Scripture: For all have sinned and fall short of the glory of God. (Rom. 3:23)

No booths were available. So I headed for the counter and ordered coffee. I immediately began to wilt. The man next to me could have lit New York with his breath. His clothes bore the soil of many days and probably many states. And, of course, he wanted to talk. He wanted to know what I did for a living. "I'm a pastor." I waited for his story about the preacher who ran off with the organist, but he said, "Well, you know, I ain't sinned since I spoke in tongues." I wish he'd waited for me to swallow the coffee. The waitress now had a spotted uniform.

"What?" I asked after apologizing to the woman.

"I ain't sinned now for thirty-two years," he proudly boasted as his broad smile revealed a mouthful of brown teeth. "Yeah, I've lived an immaculate life. Thanks be to God."

"Do you ever drink too much? Or swear?" I asked.

"I just enjoy the wine of God's goodness, and I do speak the truth from time to time. But that ain't sinnin'," he declared. Well, the Bible says not to answer a fool according to his folly so I gave up.

Last I checked, I still sin. In fact, God gave me a wife, two kids, and a dog to remind me that I'm human. Keep your Step Four inventory handy, and keep your Step Five skills polished. You'll need them again. Believe me.

Holy God, I know I'm not sinless. And thanks to you I'm not sinful either.

STEP SIX

Were entirely ready to have God remove all these defects of character.

*H*umble yourselves before the Lord, and he will lift you up. *(James 4:10)*

Step Six Reflections

*T*he work of Step Six is best begun with the understanding that God is a master husbandman who is at work in our lives. He has been preparing our lives like a farmer prepares soil. During the first five steps, God has been preparing us for this time. And what is this time? It is a time of new willingness on our part—a willingness to trust God. In Step Six we are plowed, prepared, and pliable. We are ready—ready for God.

In the Bible, we see many men and women who weren't ready for God's plan in the beginning. But we see God at work in their lives to prepare them. Noah wasn't ready to pioneer a new world, but God gave him 120 years to build the ark and prepare. Moses wasn't ready to lead Israel from Egypt at first, but God gave him forty years of leading sheep to prepare. David wasn't ready to rule Israel when he was first anointed, but God prepared him through Saul's cruel pursuit. Jesus wasn't ready to minister at age twelve when he debated the elders, but God gave him eighteen more years to prepare.

To expect action in Step Six is a mistake. Step Six purposely calls for no action on our part. It is a time for an internal change of heart and mind. Just as physical healing after an injury is not the result of effort on our part; so too, we cannot produce a willingness to change. God produces the willingness, and God produces the healing.

The Bible speaks of repentance as a gift from God. In the same way, the work accomplished in Step Six is a gift from God. The biblical word for repentance comes from two Greek words meaning "after" and "mind." We translate the word to mean a change in one's mind. That's what is occurring in Step Six: we are changing our minds. We are entirely ready in mind and spirit to have God remove the defects of character which have crippled and hurt us.

Step Six: *Were entirely ready to have God remove all these defects of character.*

Scripture: Therefore, prepare your minds for action; be self-controlled; set your hope fully on the grace to be given you when Jesus Christ is revealed. (1 Pet. 1:13)

I have a problem with one part of the above verse: ". . . be self-controlled. . . ." It seems contradictory, even mutually exclusive, to be self-controlled and to be hoping in grace in the same verse. I did research in the original language. The word for "self-controlled" is best translated "sober" or "on alert." The ancient metaphor on which this word is based recalls the picture of a dog with its ears perked.

I take my dog Good Girl, a German shepherd mix, on a walk every day. In anticipation of the walk, she constantly watches for signals and vigilantly surveys my every move. If I should put on my walking shoes, she begins to dance with hope that the walk is imminent. And when I reach for her leash, she loses all ladylike gentility as she joyfully storms through the house like a tornado.

The point is simple: Peter is telling us to remain hopefully focused on Jesus just as my pup expectantly and vigilantly watches me. In Step Six, I am at a place where my pain, power-lessness, defects, self-awareness, and exhaustion have taught me to hope entirely in God's salvation, not my own. My ears are perked, my mind sober, and my hope is set on Jesus, who alone is coming to save me. Good Girl is anxiously awaiting her walk, and I am "entirely ready" for God's help.

Master, my eyes look up. I have no self-control, but I have you.

Step Six: Were entirely ready to have God remove all these defects of character.

Scripture: Delight yourself in the Lord and he will give you the desires of your heart. Commit your way to the Lord; trust in him and he will do this. (Ps. 37:4–5)

"*D*elight" is a fairly foreign word for many in recovery. "Melancholy" is more like it. It's hard to delight in anything. Even if things go well for a while, we can't seem to enjoy them because we are just waiting for life to sour again.

In spite of my melancholy, I'm learning to delight in the Lord. But not "delight" in the skipping-for-joy sense. I'm delighted because I'm pleased and relieved to have help. I'm delighted to trust someone other than myself.

Recently, when my brother-in-law visited us with his new truck, he accidentally locked his keys inside. Of course I knew how to get his door open. I tried for an hour with a clothes hanger, and I nearly ruined the rubber strip at the window's base. I couldn't do it. So I finally gave up, exhausted and embarrassed. What a wonderful sight when the auto club truck pulled up!

That's what Step Six is like. By the time we finished with steps one to five, we're embarrassed and exhausted. And we're utterly ready for God to remove our defects and flaws. Therein lies the delight. When we have been through the wringer of moral inventory and admission, we're ready for relief.

I may not skip with delight, but I noticed a smile the other day.

Lord, my life is locked tight with my failing and faults.
Rescue me.

Step Six: ***Were entirely ready to have God remove all these defects of character.***

Scripture: *Not that I have already obtained all this, or have already been made perfect, but I press on to take hold of that for which Christ Jesus took hold of me. Brothers, I do not consider myself yet to have taken hold of it. But one thing I do: Forgetting what is behind and straining toward what is ahead, I press on toward the goal to win the prize for which God has called me heavenward in Christ Jesus. (Phil. 3:12–14)*

My seven-year-old son R.J. is an artist. Whenever he brings his masterpieces to our attention, we praise his efforts, acknowledge his creativity, and marvel at his work. He knows he's becoming a great artist. And because of his great hope in his own future, R.J. is not discouraged by minor setbacks.

For instance, I interrupted R.J. in the midst of some great creation with Lego® blocks one day. He sprang into action to protect his work from my eyes. "I'm not done yet. Go away. I'll show you when I'm ready." So I went into the bedroom to read. In a little while, R.J. proudly strutted in with his yellow and red masterpiece.

"My, R.J.," I began, "that's a beautiful . . . uh . . . uh . . ."

"It's a giraffe, of course!" he came back. And then the long neck broke off. I expressed my sorrow for his loss, but R.J. simply and unemotionally said, "That's okay. I still got a lot of work to do on this."

Like my son, the artist, we know that there is a goal, a prize, waiting ahead for us. God has given us hope and encouragement about ourselves. We know we're not perfect now, but we're on the road to better days. God has told us that we can make it, and so we will—one day at a time.

Heavenly Father, thank you for your encouragement. I'm not perfect, but with your help, I don't have to be.

Step Six: *Were entirely ready to have God remove all these defects of character.*

Scripture: *Do not conform any longer to the pattern of this world, but be transformed by the renewing of your mind. Then you will be able to test and approve what God's will is—his good, pleasing and perfect will. (Rom. 12:2)*

I hadn't known anybody like Kay. She was so colorful and in love with life. There was a freshness about her way and an excitement in her step. I loved her and opened myself to her. In time, I began to pick up her mannerisms and ways. She liked hats, so I bought one. She enjoyed live plays in the city, so I went with her. She liked dancing, so I learned. I loved her, so I wanted to share common interests, but we were from different worlds. I came from the cornfield; she came from the city. I was rough; she was refined. However, love made the difference and united us. Love made us appreciate each other and please each other.

Our relationship with God is like a love relationship. As we draw closer to the Lord, he wants more of us, and we want more of him. Then as we give ourselves to God, he gives himself back in the form of godly desires and knowledge of his will. In time, we naturally enjoy doing what pleases him. We even abandon old ways that don't fit in our new relationship with God. And that's what Step Six ought to be about: love, relationship, and change.

They say, over the years, married folks start to act, think, and even look alike. I guess it's my fate and my hope to become more like Kay and God.

God, as I draw nearer to you and abandon my old ways, please show me yourself: your desires and your will.

Step Six: *Were entirely ready to have God remove all these defects of character.*

Scripture: *Humble yourselves before the Lord, and he will lift you up. (James 4:10)*

I was to speak for a prayer fellowship, but before the service began, the woman in charge invited me for pre-service prayer. The leaders were already praying as I entered the room. I joined the circle of laymen and quietly listened. Until that moment I had known little about the fellowship, but their prayers revealed a great deal. The leader lifted her voice to a shout as she demanded in prayer. She told God that he was obliged to do miracles in their service. She began to tell God everything she expected him to do that evening. She spoke to God as if he were some heavenly butler. I wondered if she spoke to her family that way, and I began to feel awkward about my role in all this.

My message was about God's desire to see us grow and leave behind our immature ways. I reminded them that God is like a good father who knows best. I even dared suggested that our best prayers are the humble ones in which we submit to God's plan for us. Believe it or not, the group seemed to respond. But the leader didn't.

She met me afterward and told me that I wouldn't be invited back again. She told me that I had a lot to learn about walking in the Spirit. I'm sure she was right. I have a lot to learn from God, but I'll never learn it unless I'm humble enough to listen.

Heavenly Father, I humble myself best when I'm listening. Help me to hear you.

Step Six: Were entirely ready to have God remove all these defects of character.

Scripture: If any of you lacks wisdom, he should ask God, who gives generously to all without finding fault, and it will be given to him. But when he asks, he must believe and not doubt, because he who doubts is like a wave of the sea, blown and tossed by the wind. (James 1:5–6)

Michelle stared straight ahead and sat still in the lively service. The worship leader annoyed Michelle with his repetitive questions: "How many love God tonight? Isn't God good?" As the congregation loudly responded, Michelle mocked. Inside her mind and emotions she had doubts. She knew that life wasn't as simple as these people seemed to think. In real life people suffer—she suffered. She had a different set of questions: Does God really care? Where is he? Is he able to do anything? Can he help me?

While the crowd continued to praise, Michelle bowed her head. Tears spotted her slacks and mascara blackened her cheeks. She started to leave when someone sat beside her and tenderly touched her frail and bent shoulders. A radiant face, outlined with wrinkles and marked with concern, now looked at Michelle. The mature woman gently led Michelle to a quiet room where she patiently listened to Michelle's fears, struggles, doubts, and pain. And when she had finished, the two women wept and hugged. Michelle left that night with a new friend and renewed faith. God now had a face—radiant, wrinkled, and real. God heard Michelle's doubts, turned them into prayers, and sent help.

In Step Six we want God's help, but we may still have doubts about his concern. That's okay. Speak the doubts, he hears them too.

Caring God, I know that you hear my doubts as well as my prayers.

Step Six: Were entirely ready to have God remove all these defects of character.

Scripture: But the Lord is faithful, and he will strengthen and protect you from the evil one. (2 Thess. 3:3)

God gave me a wife with money sense to compensate for my lack of judgment with finances. But what seems like a good marital balance can actually be a great stress producer as well. I have always figured that you need to seize the moment and enjoy the day. And if there is not enough money to do what life is calling for today, borrow it from tomorrow. Use the money now and worry about the consequences later. Except when the "later" came, my wife was alone with the bills.

This all came to a head when I first worked Step Six. As I look back at my journal during those days, I'm reminded of how God changed my attitude about money. God opened my eyes to see how my irresponsibility hurt my wife and family. My poor judgment hurt the ones I love, and that, in turn, hurt me. I suddenly had the perfect picture of a jerk. I saw him every time I looked in the mirror. Believe me, I learned what it meant to be "entirely ready" to have God remove a defect.

God can strengthen and protect us from the evil one on the outside, and he can protect us from the evil that dwells within. God knows how to get our attention with the help of the loved ones who are closest to us. When we see the pain that our defects cause others, we see the need for God's help.

God, thank you for making me ready to change.

Step Six: Were entirely ready to have God remove all these defects of character.

Scripture: In the same way, count yourselves dead to sin but alive to God in Christ Jesus. Therefore do not let sin reign in your mortal body so that you obey its evil desires. (Rom. 6:11–12)

*T*he funeral was well under way. The family was seated. The organist had just played the deceased's favorite hymn. The pastor approached the pulpit to speak, "Now is the time for which we have all been waiting. The deceased will give his final farewell." The pastor turned to the casket with the microphone. The deceased lifted his stiff form up to speak. He took the microphone and thanked the pastor.

"Thank you all so much for coming today. I'm sure I'll miss each one of you. Remember to keep the faith, encourage one another, and be happy. Bye, Mom." The deceased then returned the microphone, reclined in the coffin, folded his hands, and closed his eyes for the last time.

Does this all seem silly? You bet! But why? Because when you are literally dead to the world, you can't communicate with the world. In the same way, when you are dead to sin, you can't relate to it anymore. You can't speak to sin, and you can't hear sin's call. You're in another world: God's kingdom. But none of this is possible until you are entirely ready for God to change your address to his kingdom and your life to his control.

I don't know about you, but I'm tired of sin's call on my life. I'm ready to turn a deaf ear to sin, to be dead to it.

Dear God, I'm weary of sin's effect. I'm tired of my defects. Please take me to a better place in you.

Step Six: *Were entirely ready to have God remove all these defects of character.*

Scripture: *This is the assurance we have in approaching God: that is if we ask anything according to his will, he hears us. And if we know that he hears us—whatever we ask—we know that we have what we asked of him. (1 John 5:14–15)*

The yellow cab deposited Gramps at the curb. He lumbered toward the house, suitcase in one hand, satchel in the other. Steve kept his eye on the satchel because it held the gifts. This time the satchel offered up a red truck that Steve took right to the dirt pile. The truck worked hard for several minutes before Steve noticed a missing wheel. No amount of looking helped. The wheel had disappeared. Then Gramps came out to see the toy in action.

Steve was frightened. All he could think about was how his dad would react if he found out. He would slap his head and call him stupid. "Damn you! Get a brain!" he'd say. Dad would shame him for losing something his grandpa had paid good money for.

"How's the truck work, Steve?" Gramps asked.

"Real good, Gramps. Thanks." But Steve never looked up. Then Gramps bent down to show Steve a special feature, and he saw the missing wheel. Steve froze.

"Oops, what happened?" Gramps asked. "Looks like we lost a wheel. Let me help you look for it."

Steve feared his benevolent grandpa because his father taught him to fear and to feel shame. But his grandpa wasn't like his dad. In the same way, we sometimes fear God because of the abuse of our parents. But God is good. He won't shame or slap or swear. Go ahead, approach him.

Heavenly Father, here's my broken life. Please help.

STEP SEVEN

*Humbly asked him
to remove our
shortcomings.*

*I*f we confess our sins, he is
faithful and just and will forgive
us our sins and purify us from
all unrighteousness. *(1 John 1:9)*

Step Seven Reflections

*H*umility is the key to success in Step Seven. And humility is best modeled for us in God's nature as seen in Christ. Jesus did something that scholars call *kenosis* or "emptying." Although Jesus was, in fact, God, he emptied himself and came to us as a servant. Jesus humbly approached the world. He did not come as superior or special; he came as a servant. The sinless Son of God laid aside his special rights and his special powers in order to approach us and serve. He could have come in rightful superiority and pride, but he didn't.

We who are in recovery also need to approach someone—we need to approach God. But unlike Jesus, we don't come sinlessly. We approach God with the knowledge of our shortcomings. And if Christ didn't approach us in pride, we must not approach him in pride. We must see our own faults and not compare ourselves with others. We must come emptied and without haughtiness. We must come in powerlessness, recognizing our needs before God.

The first six steps have prepared us for this time. Our hearts have been plowed and exposed. Now is the time for humble prayer.

But many of us don't know how to pray—period. So humble prayer is even more of a task or mystery. The most sincere prayer that can be prayed in Step Seven is the simple and genuine cry of our hearts for help.

Just as we called out for our parents to help us as children, we call out for God's help. We have tried on our own, and we have failed. Now with a sense of our powerlessness and our need, having been humbled by our shortcomings and sin, we lift our hearts heavenward for help.

Step Seven: Humbly asked him to remove our shortcomings.

Scripture: *Good and upright is the Lord; therefore he instructs sinners in his ways. He guides the humble in what is right and teaches them his way. All the ways of the Lord are loving and faithful for those who keep the demands of his covenant. For the sake of your name, O Lord, forgive my iniquity, though it is great. (Ps. 25:8–11)*

I know just enough about car repairs to be dangerous. I chose not to learn when Dad offered. It started when my brother and I were kids. We each decided to build soapbox cars for our own derby. I knew that I could do it on my own, but Rex asked Dad for help. We both had the same wood, wheels, and will, but Rex had Dad and the humility to learn.

When we were done, we took our cars to the top of the hill. Dad stood at the bottom to start the race. As Rex settled in behind his steering wheel, he pretended to start his engine and adjust his imaginary goggles. He snarled, "Eat my dust!" As I settled into my chariot, the wheels leaned inward and the whole car creaked. Then Dad dropped his hand, and the race was on. In a flurry of laughter and squeals, Rex's car flew down the hill. Dad was already cheering and patting Rex on the back when my car finally started to roll. Dad later said my problem was "no axle." How was I to know? I figured big nails would hold the wheels on!

Life is a lot more complicated than preparing for a soapbox derby. Our defects and shortcomings aren't easily fixed. We need God's help. But that's okay because God wants to help—he stands ready to help. All we need do is humbly ask.

Heavenly Father, I want to build a life that will really fly. Will you help me?

Step Seven: Humbly asked him to remove our shortcomings.

Scripture: Do not be anxious about anything, but in everything, by prayer and petition, with thanksgiving, present your requests to God. (Phil. 4:6)

*M*y whole life seemed to be falling apart. Emotionally, spiritually, and physically I was a wreck. As an adult child, I really didn't think that I could sort things out for myself. So I drove over a hundred miles to get sympathy and encouragement from an older friend. However, in my impulsiveness, I neglected to call him first. He was out of town. So I drove another twenty-five miles further just to find that my second choice was also out of town. I felt defeated as I started the journey home.

Out of desperation I decided to pray. God was now my last resort instead of my first hope. As I began to pray, the Lord brought my whole life to mind. I recalled how he protected me in childhood, how he guarded me during military service, and how he carried me through difficult college years. I remembered how he gave me a wife and many good friends, how he kept food on our table and a roof over our heads, how he provided work to do and good health. I remembered how God has always taken care of me, even in the tough times. Somehow he has always pulled me through. Then I heard the Lord say to my troubled heart, "And I won't abandon you now."

God really is able to quiet our anxiousness when we take the time to pray. And God wants prayer to be our first hope, not our last resort.

God, help me remember that one of my shortcomings is not bringing my troubled heart to you.

Step Seven: Humbly asked him to remove our shortcomings.

Scripture: *If we confess our sins, he is faithful and just and will forgive us our sins and purify us from all unrighteousness. (1 John 1:9)*

*F*or Chuck's friends, life was a party and every night was an opportunity for alcohol, drugs, and sex. But something inside Chuck was changing. He began to feel uncomfortable with his life-style and friends. Chuck would stay awake at night and pray. He would pray "forgive me" over and over as if pure repetition would get God's attention. But nothing ever changed. He'd be out the next night doing the same things.

Then one day, an old friend reappeared in his life, but the old friend was changed. His life was cleaned up, and he seemed really happy, not happy merely because he was loaded. This friend told Chuck that Christ had made the difference in his life. At first Chuck resisted, but he knew this was what he needed to hear. Within a few hours the old friend had Chuck praying again, not just crying "forgive me." Chuck told God his faults and humbly asked him to cleanse him and change his life. This time Chuck meant it, and God answered.

We can all cry out in our pain. Our shortcomings and defects hurt us, but just crying "ouch" or "forgive me" is not enough. God is waiting for us to humbly ask him to do more. He's waiting for our confession and our humble request for cleansing. "Ouch" is a good place to start, but it's not enough.

Holy God, here are my sins. I humbly ask your forgiveness and your cleansing.

Step Seven: Humbly asked him to remove our shortcomings.

Scripture: For whoever exalts himself will be humbled, and whoever humbles himself will be exalted. (Matt. 23:12)

*T*he church's one-hundred-year history was seasoned by the influence of the Heidelbecks, and Mrs. Heidelbeck was proud of her historic position in the church. But the new crowd of parishioners alarmed her. The pastor had been attracting the wrong "sort," in her opinion, and Mr. Fox was her least favorite.

The whole Fox family drove to church in an old beat-up truck, and Mr. Fox was a lot like his truck. He wore outdated suits, chain smoked, and barely provided for his family. The county once threatened to sell his house for taxes, but he got his truck working in time to get a steady job. Somehow they always made it to church.

Mrs. Heidelbeck told Mr. Fox that his presence in the church affected the church's image. "People like you give the wrong signal. I don't mean any of this personally, of course," she said, "but you must understand. Don't you?" Mr. Fox understood all too well. He left the church, and the pastor soon followed. By the end of that year the church fell to thirty members. One family remained: the Heidelbecks. Great image!

One way to determine our humility is to measure how tolerant we are of others, especially the lowly. We learn humility before God by practicing on those around us and by remembering Jesus. Although he was God, he humbled himself and came to us.

God, help me learn humility from your example, not from my mistakes.

Step Seven: *Humbly asked him to remove our shortcomings.*

Scripture: But he gives us more grace. That is why Scripture says: "God opposes the proud but gives grace to the humble." Submit yourselves, then, to God. Resist the devil, and he will flee from you. Come near to God and he will come near to you. Wash your hands, you sinners, and purify your hearts, you double-minded. (James 4:6–8)

*H*e always comes late to the meeting. He misses the instruction time and never seems to listen to others. He can't wait until he can talk. He tells us how awful his wife is and how sick he is. He is so persecuted and downtrodden—pathetic. No one at work understands his struggles. And if he should slip and come to a meeting with alcohol on his breath, well, who can blame him? His prayer list takes an eternity to recite. And we're all supposed to feel sorry for him.

In our addiction, many of us exercise a false humility that is designed to elicit grace and sympathy from others—even from God. We try to make people feel sorry for us: We weren't dealt a fair hand in life. It's not our fault if we fail. We were doomed to fail—our fate made it so. And so our unfortunate circumstances in life give us the right to feel sorry for ourselves and to expect special treatment from others.

But this addictive insanity is not humility. God doesn't give grace because we manipulate him. He gives grace to the humble because they freely admit their need and trust him for the answer. We have lived many years getting what we want through manipulation, but it won't work with God. Humility obtains grace, and submission gains God's favor.

God, forgive me for manipulating you and others. Teach me to humbly draw near.

Step Seven: Humbly asked him to remove our shortcomings.

Scripture: *Create in me a pure heart, O God, and renew a steadfast spirit within me. Do not cast me from your presence or take your Holy Spirit from me. Restore to me the joy of your salvation and grant me a willing spirit, to sustain me. (Ps. 51:10–12)*

King David of Israel wrote this prayer when his sin had been revealed to him. Because many of us seek our self-worth in the opinion of others, we fear that when we sin or make a mistake we will lose our friends, loved ones, and God. David prayed, "Do not cast me from your presence. . . ." In essence he said, "Don't throw me away."

I know of a woman who was literally thrown in the fire on the day of her birth because her father wanted a boy. This woman lost a leg from severe burns, but she lost more than a part of her body. She lost her right to feel worth. She was told from her earliest days that she was unacceptable, not good enough.

We are all a bit like King David. We worry when we make mistakes and sin. We worry that we might be thrown out with the trash. We can even feel like trash when we listen to the condemning voices inside. But please learn with me what King David learned: God doesn't throw away sinners. He redeems them, forgives them, and heals them. Sinners are valuable to God, not because of what they do, but because of whose they are. They are his.

God won't throw us away. He gave everything to save us.

Forgiving Lord, when I sin, you don't cast me away; you draw me near. Thank you.

Step Seven: Humbly asked him to remove our shortcomings.

Scripture: Humble yourselves, therefore, under God's mighty hand, that he may lift you up in due time. Cast all your anxiety on him because he cares for you. (1 Pet. 5:6–7)

Aaron and his law school roommate were different as night and day. The bright and well-heeled roomie was bred from New England's finest, and he embodied the Ivy League type. Aaron was from more common stock, and he was admitted to school only because of a special scholarship program for underprivileged students. His single mother cleaned floors in order to help him with living expenses. But greatest among Aaron's struggles was his sight. He was severely nearsighted and needed to hold a book just a few inches from his eyes in order to read.

Aaron's roommate had been blessed with excellent vision and a photographic memory. Late at night, when Aaron studied, his roommate partied. Aaron's roomie would look in his books at the last minute, memorize what he needed, and go to class. Aaron was not as gifted, but he humbly tried and honorably toiled day after day. And Aaron asked God's help to rise above his disabilities.

On graduation day, Aaron's roommate was absent and his well-heeled family had no reason to be proud. But there was a very proud mother in the crowd that day. The mother had callused knees and coarse hands. And although her son found it difficult to see his mother in the crowd, he knew she was there.

Like Aaron, we in recovery face challenges that others do not, but with God's help we can rise above and succeed as we humbly ask for God's help.

Caring Lord, I can't succeed without your help. Please help me rise above my shortcomings.

Step Seven: Humbly asked him to remove our shortcomings.

Scripture: Have mercy on me, O God, according to your unfailing love; according to your great compassion blot out my transgressions. Wash away all my iniquity and cleanse me from my sin. (Ps. 51:1–2)

I have a problem that won't die easily. Whenever I am quiet, past mistakes and failures parade before my conscious mind, and before I can stop the thoughts, I have already verbally and mentally berated myself. For example, the uninvited memory of a stupid remark to a superior will pop up. Then before I know what has happened, I will say to myself, "You stupid idiot! Why did you ever say that?" Or I will remember when I belittled a coworker. Or when I accidentally hurt my son. Whatever the memory, I always scold myself without mercy. Sometimes, when a condemning memory has been recalled, I can't easily forget it; it will follow me through the day.

I know part of the reason why it hurts. I care too much about what others think. I fear that my stupid mistakes have irreparably damaged their opinion of me. So I punish myself as if the punishment could atone for the mistakes. But in recovery I'm learning to get my sense of worth from God and his opinion of me. In God, I find mercy, not scolding.

I'm learning to face the mistakes and to admit to their existence. I admit my powerlessness over the past, and I humbly ask God to remove my shortcomings. The habit dies hard, but when I humbly bring the mistakes to God, he shows me mercy and takes some of the sting out.

Merciful God, you know my past mistakes. I humbly ask for the mercy and grace to forgive myself.

Step Seven: Humbly asked him to remove our shortcomings.

Scripture: Repent, then, and turn to God, so that your sins may be wiped out, that times of refreshing may come from the Lord. (Acts 3:19)

*H*ere is the poem of an adult child who has had to face shortcomings and sins far older than himself:

> I saw my dad the other day
> although he's been gone for years.
> He scolded and shamed my children
> and filled them with panic and fear.
> He shouted until his veins popped out
> and controlled them with his threats.
> He left them crying and hurting
> and mumbled, "I'm not through with you yet."
> I saw my dad the other day and
> wished with all my heart he'd stay
> In his cold and forgotten grave
> and let us live our lives our way.
> I don't want to see him anymore
> or feel his judging heart.
> Please God, let us stop repeating history
> and let us make a new start.

The Bible says that the sins of the father are visited to the third and fourth generations. We are powerless over sin and its control, but God is not. In his grace, God has allowed us to see our sin and even its origins, but we cannot remove these failings on our own. Only God can remove sin. And only we can humbly ask him to do it.

When we see our shortcomings, faults, defects, and sins, we don't make excuses, don't blame the past, don't even determine to do better. We simply and humbly take the failure and sin to God and ask him to remove it.

Eternal God, some sins have been in my family for generations. I repent for them all.

STEP EIGHT

Made a list of all persons we had harmed, and became willing to make amends to them all.

Do to others as you would have them do to you. *(Luke 6:31)*

Step Eight Reflections

When we approach Step Eight, we remember something about God that we focused on in Step Six: God is a master husbandman who is at work in our lives. He has prepared our lives like a farmer prepares soil. God has used the first seven steps to prepare us for this time. And what is this time? It is a time for willingness on our part to accept responsibility for our past. With the help of our Step Four inventory, we recognize that we are responsible for our situations in life. And we recognize that we have harmed other people.

Like Step Six, we have needed time to become accustomed to this new willingness. We have spent a lifetime blaming all our troubles on others. We have made others feel responsible for our grief and suffering. We have made others suffer along with us. But God, in his graciousness, has allowed us to slowly change and become comfortable with the truth that we—and no one else—are the ones who need to change. We cannot change others, but we can face ourselves and own up to our responsibility.

In Step Eight, God will bring the names and faces of others to mind. We must be careful not to say, "Well, they hurt me more than I hurt them." Step Eight is not about them; it is about us. We are taking responsibility for what we did. God's Word tells us to do to others as we would have them do to us.

While working Step Eight, we must be careful not to take any shortcuts. There is great wisdom in a separate step just for reflection and for making a list of persons we have harmed. During this time, God is again working inside our hearts and minds. He is making us willing to face our mistakes and preparing us to make amends. He is strengthening our foundation so that Step Nine will be meaningful and life changing.

Scripture: But Zacchaeus stood up and said to the Lord, "Look, Lord! Here and now I give half of my possessions to the poor, and if I have cheated anybody out of anything, I will pay back four times the amount." (Luke 19:8)

*F*our-year-old R.J. had explored and conquered every toy on the playground; so we figured it was time for lunch. I dumped a mountain of sand from each shoe and securely buckled him in the car seat. "Where do you want to go for lunch, R.J.?" I asked. "Do you want to go to Taco Bell, Burger King, McDonald's, or Taco Bell?"

"McDonald's!" came the enthusiastic reply.

"Well now, are you sure? Do you want Taco Bell, McDonald's, Taco Bell, Burger King, Taco Bell, McDonald's, or Taco Bell?" I asked again.

"McDonald's!" came the reply.

"But are you sure? Do you want Taco Bell, McDonald's, Taco Bell, or Taco Bell?" I asked one more time.

"Taco Bell," R.J. finally responded.

"Well great!" I said. "Good choice."

Once I saw my defects and failings and once I began to make a list of persons I had harmed, I realized that I had often cheated my own son by manipulating his choices and by putting words into his mouth. In so doing, I taught him that his thoughts weren't important and his choices didn't count.

Manipulation of others may be subtle or obvious, but it is always wrong.

Lord, I see now how I have harmed others through manipulation. Help me correct it.

Step Eight: *Made a list of all persons we had harmed, and became willing to make amends to them all.*

Scripture: *Dear friends, since God so loved us, we also ought to love one another. No one has ever seen God; but if we love one another, God lives in us and his love is made complete in us. (1 John 4:11–12)*

I often hang around our local marina, but I don't know anybody there because I tend to avoid contact with others. During one of my visits, I went into the snack bar for a soda. As I entered the snack bar, I noticed an elderly man with a cane standing motionlessly near a bench. His statuelike appearance was odd, but I thought nothing of it. As I left the snack bar, I noticed a younger man standing next to the older man. "Are you okay, Hank?" he asked.

Hank answered, but he spoke very slowly and softly. "I can't seem to move."

"It's that damned Parkinson's disease, isn't it, Hank?" the younger man asked. But old Hank couldn't answer. A tear of frustration spoke for him. "Here, let me get you home." So the man pulled up his truck and tenderly carried Hank home.

As I returned to the car, my emotions were near the surface (my dad had Parkinson's). I couldn't help but cry tears of sympathy for old Hank, tears of thanks for the younger man, and tears of loneliness for myself. Hank had friends who loved him. I had no one. I've blamed everyone around me for my pain, but my blaming brings me only isolation. I want to love people again—I need people. But I can only reconnect to people by working Step Eight, by taking responsibility for my actions, by becoming willing to make amends, and not by blaming.

God, help me love people again, and not blame them for my own mistakes.

Step Eight: Made a list of all persons we had harmed, and became willing to make amends to them all.

Scripture: For if you forgive men when they sin against you, your heavenly Father will also forgive you. But if you do not forgive men their sins, your Father will not forgive your sins. (Matt. 6:14–15)

At the request of a friend, I visited a woman who had attempted suicide. She approached wearing a bathrobe, and her hair was a mess. Around each wrist were bandages. Her pain had taken her capacity for courteous conversation. "Who are you, and what do you want?" she demanded.

After I explained that I was a pastor, she said, "Every pastor I know is a liar or an actor. Which are you? And churches only care about money. They're all sanctimonious hypocrites who don't give a damn about anybody but themselves! Now what have you got to say?" I just stared at my Bible.

Although I had never attempted suicide, I knew what it was to hate the Church, God, and myself. This woman's pain and unforgiveness were an open book. When I finally lifted my eyes to hers, I said, "I'm glad that most of the Psalms have some element of complaint. There's a lot to complain about in life." She began to soften, and over the next hour, I heard her complaint. When she was done I prayed a simple petition for grace: forgiveness for faulty humanity.

A few months later, this woman came to church. She said, "Thanks for not being offended by my behavior."

God knows that before we can forgive or be forgiven we must vent our feelings. That's why there's prayer. God hears our complaint and extends the grace we need to forgive.

Forgiving God, hear my complaint, see my unforgiveness, and heal my agony.

Scripture: You therefore, have no excuse, you who pass judgment on someone else, for at whatever point you judge the other, you are condemning yourself, because you who pass judgment do the same things. (Rom. 2:1)

I know a man named Carl who was fired from every job he ever had—some twenty-one jobs. Some jobs only lasted a few days. His longest lasted eighteen months. In every case, Carl could describe how his firing was someone else's fault. He always lost his jobs because someone else didn't understand him, bosses asked for too much, fellow workers took advantage of him, or the jobs were too hard for too little pay. It was never his fault. He finally moved north to greener pastures.

Carl once told me that his father, "a good Christian man," regularly and severely beat him with a strap until Carl left home at the age of seventeen to escape the punishment. Somehow I wasn't surprised when I found Carl's teenage daughter in a Twelve-Step group for youth. She had run away from Carl's greener pastures and traveled six hundred miles on her own to live with her aunt. The girl spoke tearfully of her dad and said, "He's never wrong! It's always my fault!"

So long as we judge and evaluate the defects and shortcomings of others, we will never have to face our own. It's time to think about the people we have hurt, not to blame them.

Righteous God, you alone are righteous enough to judge.

Step Eight: *Made a list of all persons we had harmed, and became willing to make amends to them all.*

Scripture: *But I tell you who hear me: Love your enemies, do good to those who hate you, bless those who curse you, pray for those who mistreat you.* *(Luke 6:27–28)*

*N*egro spirituals have long been a source of spiritual wisdom and emotional strength. They are the expression of broken hearts that have been mended by God's hope and love.

> I love ev'rybody, I love ev'rybody,
> I love ev'rybody in my heart.
> I love Hoss Manucy, I love Hoss Manucy,
> I love Hoss Manucy in my heart.

After this verse had been sung, somebody would undoubtedly object because it was hard to sing about love for Hoss Manucy when he'd beat them. Someone else would counter that Hoss was still a human with some degree of dignity in the sight of God. "We don't have to like him, but we have to love him. He's been damaged too."* And so they would sing and love even the people who mistreated and abused.

The black slaves knew what it was to be abused. We in recovery have been abused and mistreated too. During those times we were powerless to defend ourselves, powerless to retaliate, and powerless to change our situation. But we were not then nor are we now powerless to love and forgive. God gives that power.

In the Negro spiritual, some justified their need to love Hoss Manucy by saying, "He's been damaged too." And that's true in our lives as well. Those who hurt us were damaged victims of abuse. Loving one's enemies releases the hate, frees God to work, and stops the chain of abuse.

God, I want to love everybody in my heart.

*From *Freedom Is a Constant Struggle*, edited by Guy and Candie Carawan, NY: Oak Publications, 1968.

Step Eight: *Made a list of all persons we had harmed, and became willing to make amends to them all.*

Scripture: Do not judge, and you will not be judged. Do not condemn, and you will not be condemned. Forgive, and you will be forgiven. Give, and it will be given to you. A good measure, pressed down, shaken together and running over, will be poured into your lap. For with the measure you use, it will be measured to you. (Luke 6:37–38)

*T*he dreaded intersection was crowded. It had a notoriously short left-turn arrow. And I was now stuck behind a slowpoke in a tiny car. He didn't look very alert, and I was sure that he wouldn't turn fast enough. I was right. When the arrow turned green, his car slowly crept ahead with uneven jerks and jolts. I growled as I rode his bumper in angry defiance. The light turned yellow, then red, and we were caught in the middle as opposing traffic began to crowd and honk.

When we finally cleared the embarrassment and exasperation of the intersection, I postured my car to come alongside this inconsiderate slowpoke. I wouldn't do anything obscene, but I would give him a nasty look. I pulled alongside with my ugly face in place when I saw his handicapped sticker. He was driving his specially equipped car with only his upper arms and teeth. There was no time to change my face into a smile because it had already changed into shock and embarrassment.

The way I had judged this man long before I knew the facts was the story of my life. I had blamed everyone around me for getting in my way and disturbing my progress. I had selfishly run over many good people. I needed to face my own selfishness, and I needed to be willing to face the people I'd hurt. I've learned that my real handicap isn't anyone but me.

Gracious God, give me the grace to forgive myself and others without judging first.

Step Eight: Made a list of all persons we had harmed, and became willing to make amends to them all.

Scripture: Be kind and compassionate to one another, forgiving each other, just as in Christ God forgave you. (Eph. 4:32)

*T*he letter spoke of a mother's care for her young son and a woman's concern over her estranged husband. "Don't forget to change his underwear. And be sure he eats. The taverns are no place for a boy." I don't know how she ever allowed young Elmer to travel from Chicago to Detroit with his alcoholic father, but she did.

As I read the brown and brittle pages of the ancient letter, I couldn't help but feel compassion for the boy. The permanent marks on his legs told the story of punishment from his father, a Chicago street-car conductor. The same street-car strap that marked Elmer's back and legs had also marred his mother's fair skin. Elmer grew up knowing anger and beatings, arguing and persecution, alcoholism and poverty. He was robbed of childhood. Pain took the place of play, and fear displaced fun.

Tears now marked the pages of the letter. I carefully folded it and placed it back in my grandma's aged and cracked purse. My dad, who is now gone, would never have showed his mother's letters, but I found them among old boxes.

My dad was a victim. It is easier to feel compassion for my dad and forgive when I remember his pain and remember his struggle. Many of us who are in recovery were damaged by parents. Compassion begins with our ability to see their pain. I hope my children extend that grace to me.

Forgiving Father, give me compassion for those who have harmed me.

Step Eight: Made a list of all persons we had harmed, and became willing to make amends to them all.

Scripture: We who are strong ought to bear with the failings of the weak and not to please ourselves. Each of us should please his neighbor for his good, to build him up. For even Christ did not please himself, but, as it is written: "The insults of those who insulted you have fallen on me." (Rom. 15:1–3)

The preacher got laughs. He said, "What a convenient excuse for failing in life. Just say that you came from a dysfunctional home and that your mother screwed your diapers on too tight. If you just get your heart right with God and stop whining about what size diapers your mother used, you'll be okay." Everyone around me chuckled. But I didn't. And I couldn't help but think that the crowd laughed to keep from crying.

Laughing at folks who struggle with the wounds of their past is not building them up. It is, in fact, tearing them down and probably something to make amends for. We who are in recovery need to live as examples of compassion and concern for the hurting. Our example begins when we show a willingness to accept responsibility for ourselves and when we demonstrate a willingness to consider the injury we've caused others. And by our example of ultimately making amends, we can show others God's power of healing.

People who are hurting need our fellowship and love to show them God's love. They don't need anyone to tell them to stop whining. In Twelve-Step meetings, I've seen burdens lifted, the weak made strong, and people built up. When we look with compassion on others and see them as real people, it's easier to want to make things right between us.

Compassionate God, you see me as a real person with real needs. Help me see others in the same way.

Step Eight: Made a list of all persons we had harmed, and became willing to make amends to them all.

Scripture: Why do you look at the speck of sawdust in your brother's eye and pay no attention to the plank in your own eye? How can you say to your brother, "Let me take the speck out of your eye," when all the time there is a plank in your own eye? (Matt. 7:3–4)

*T*aylor and his wife had attended services for about a month when he told me he loved our church. He was sure that he and his wife would be happy in our congregation. But then he recited a long litany of churches he had attended and left. He explained how each church or pastor had offended him. None of the other churches were good enough, but ours was different. "Yeah, right!" I thought.

Later, he told me about an ex-wife and daughter who didn't deserve the child support he was supposed to pay. In fact, he said that if they attached his wages, he would quit his job. It was time he found a new job anyway.

Taylor didn't stay long at our church. He told me that I had offended him by not allowing him to speak or teach publicly. He was a gifted leader, and I was obviously conceited and jealous. In the year following his exodus from our church, he was offended by two more churches. He finally started a church in his home. It ended after about six months when some attendees offended Taylor by questioning his harsh treatment of his new wife. He sent them all away, including his wife.

I can't speak for Taylor, but I know I have acted just as insanely. You know what I found? As long as I'm blaming, I'm not recovering. Accepting my responsibility and considering the pain I've caused others marked my change.

Dear God, take the plank out of my eye, not so I can see others, but so I can see myself.

Step Eight: Made a list of all persons we had harmed, and became willing to make amends to them all.

Scripture: "And when you stand praying, if you hold anything against anyone, forgive him, so that your Father in heaven may forgive you your sins." (Mark 11:25)

O ne person has truly hurt me. He showed me no mercy and didn't let me forget any of my mistakes. He was always negative about my life and prevented me from having close friends. He kept me from God through his anxious thought and behavior. And he destroyed my health through abuse and neglect. I find it hard to think kindly of him, but I know my recovery depends upon him.

I hear him every morning. He greets me as the cobwebs of sleep are swept away by consciousness. He immediately suggests how I ought to feel or think and reminds me of my mistakes. He frightens me about possibilities and never lets me forget the worries awaiting me. He says I'm not good enough. He says that I'm lucky for having survived and that my luck is running out.

I'd be better off without this guy. His defects and shortcomings are oppressive. I've often tried to lose him, but when I wake up. . . . I've used painkillers to silence him. I've used alcohol to suppress him. I've used codependent behavior to appease him. I've even considered killing him to stop his abuse. But. . . . I hate him. Damn him.

I told God about him the other day. God said that I should forgive him. God said that he had already forgiven him and that I should too. So when he met me the other morning, I forgave him, and it felt good. I may even learn to love him—to love me.

Forgiving Lord, before I can forgive anyone, I need help to forgive myself.

STEP NINE

Made direct amends to such people wherever possible, except when to do so would injure them or others.

*T*herefore, if you are offering your gift at the altar and there remember that your brother has something against you, leave your gift there in front of the altar. First go and be reconciled to your brother; then come and offer your gift. *(Matt. 5:23–24)*

Step Nine Reflections

As we approach Step Nine, it is good to remember that God, who does not unrighteously harm another, has nevertheless provided for wrongs to be made right. The best example of this is our sin. God gave Adam and Eve a free will and with it the potential for sin. Adam and Eve chose the sin. God could have righteously condemned man for all time because of their actions, but instead he chose to make a way for restoration and redemption. God sent his only Son to make the amend. Jesus, who had no sin, became sin for us so that we could approach God again.

In Step Nine, God is asking us to approach others. He is asking us to make things right with the people we have harmed. Some of these people have harmed us as much or more than we have harmed them, but just as Jesus made amends when he was not at fault, so we must make things right even with the unrighteous and undeserving. The Bible says that while we were still in our sin, Christ died for us. And so while others may still be in denial and dysfunction, we must make amends. Step Nine is about *us,* not them. They will benefit from our courageous efforts, but we will be changed and healed.

Step Nine is a time for forgiveness, not just the forgiveness we may or may not receive from others. It is a time for us to forgive. In forgiving we relinquish control: we surrender the right to hate, to feel bitterness, to keep records of offenses, to resent, to punish. As we seek the forgiveness of others to whom we make amends, we must also be willing to forgive.

***Step Nine:** Made direct amends to such people wherever possible, except when to do so would injure them or others.*

***Scripture:** We love because he first loved us. If anyone says, "I love God," yet hates his brother, he is a liar. For anyone who does not love his brother, whom he has seen, cannot love God, whom he has not seen. (1 John 4:19–21)*

A black family visited our church two weeks in a row when choir members began murmuring that it was getting "too colorful." I publicly lashed out the next Sunday morning. One of the elders called me aside and said, "Now I believe blacks can be saved. I just don't want them in *my* church."

I made weekly visits to that same elder's bedridden father. The older man told me stories of how he abused the blacks in Oklahoma cotton fields. He even indicated that "lazy or unruly" black workers were occasionally killed as examples. As he relived his memories, his hatred for blacks spilled out like a poison. It was easy to see where his son's hatred came from.

That elder also had a son. Like his father before him, the elder imparted hate to his son. And today that elder's son is in prison for having killed a black man. He stabbed the man in the heart seven times, and he didn't even know him.

All those men, especially my elder, claimed to love God. They even felt they had the right to rule God's Church. I disagreed. I told them publicly that with such hatred they could never feel comfortable in heaven and that with such prejudice they might not be welcome.

In the same way, we who are in recovery can never claim to love God while we harbor hatred for others.

God, help me remember that the best way to show my love for you is to love others.

Step Nine: Made direct amends to such people wherever possible, except when to do so would injure them or others.

Scripture: You have heard that it was said, "Love your neighbor and hate your enemy." But I tell you, "Love your enemies and pray for those who persecute you." (Matt. 5:43–44)

I was at the end of my rope with the chief petty officer who was my supervisor on the ship. I was sure he didn't like me because I was a Christian. "Blatant prejudice," I complained. He didn't allow me to advance in rank, he didn't authorize my leave requests, he made me work harder. Finally, I went to a Christian friend who said that I should try forgiving and loving him. He said I should be kind to him and pray for him. He said I should apologize to him for any offense I may have caused. It wasn't easy, but I did it.

After weeks of showing kindness and praying for him, something changed. I was on a lonely watch during the middle of the night when he stood beside me. He had a can of soda and a smile. He said, "Thanks for all the soda you've been bringing me lately." That was all he said, but our relationship was never the same. We became very close. In fact, a few years after we were both out of the Navy, he wrote me and said, "Whatever good has ever come from my life is as a result of knowing you." I didn't deserve a comment that gracious. All I did was love an enemy. I obeyed the Bible, and it worked.

We might be surprised when we start making amends. We might see enemies transformed into friends.

God, give me courage to obey you and give me faith to expect the best from my amends.

Step Nine: Made direct amends to such people wherever possible, except when to do so would injure them or others.

Scripture: *Above all, love each other deeply, because love covers a multitude of sins. Offer hospitality to one another without grumbling. Each one should use whatever gift he has received to serve others, faithfully administering God's grace in its various forms. (1 Pet. 4:8–10)*

The wedding rehearsal was just about to begin. The sanctuary was crowded with family and friends of the bride and groom. I studied the crowd to pick out the bride's father. Although I had never met him, I had heard much about him, and I hated him. For many years he had sexually abused his daughter, a close friend of mine from work. I envisioned him as a monster, an evil-looking serpent with sinister eyes. But I saw no such man in the crowd. Then the bride came in.

She began to move toward an older man and woman. She extended her arms to the man and he did the same. It was her dad. She actually seemed to love him. Now I knew she'd forgiven him, but I didn't expect her to show affection to this monster. So I asked her about it later. She said, "I love my dad even though he hurt me. I can't change yesterday, but in God's grace I can forgive and love today." She really meant it.

Making amends cannot change yesterday, but it just might help someone forgive and love again. Our amends affect more than just ourselves for good.

God, never let me forget the power of love when I seek to make amends.

Step Nine: Made direct amends to such people wherever possible, except when to do so would injure them or others.

Scripture: Therefore, if you are offering your gift at the altar and there remember that your brother has something against you, leave your gift there in front of the altar. First go and be reconciled to your brother; then come and offer your gift. (Matt. 5:23–24)

*T*he engineer in the recording booth was helping me make a religiously oriented radio spot. When I was done she said, "You know, I could never be religious. My mother forever ruined me." She spoke with rigid defiance, and she snarled her lip when she said, "My mother." When I asked why, she explained how her mother belonged to a particular religious sect that didn't allow birthday celebrations, Christmas observances, and even flag salutes. She hissed in anger as she remembered the humiliation of being told to leave the classroom during the morning pledge of allegiance. Then she quieted her voice as she recalled her mother's absence at her wedding and her absence at the birth of her daughter. "She punished me," she said, "because I had rejected her faith. I haven't seen her in seven years."

Many of us who are in recovery find it hard to approach God because of past offenses. We can never feel free so long as there are things that need to be made right. We may go back to people we have hurt and find that they are unwilling to accept our amends, but that's okay. Before God, we have tried. The radio engineer may one day seek to make things right with her mother, and her mother may still reject her. But I know that God will honor her attempt. In fact, I told her that. I also asked her not to judge God because of her mother.

God, I want to approach you freely without the burden of unfinished business. Help me.

Step Nine: Made direct amends to such people wherever possible, except when to do so would injure them or others.

Scripture: . . . *if he gives back what he took in pledge for a loan, returns what he has stolen, follows the decrees that give life, and does no evil, he will surely live; he will not die. None of the sins he has committed will be remembered against him. He had done what is just and right; he will surely live. (Ezek. 33:15–16)*

*D*uring my first year in the Navy, I couldn't help but admire a very special Buck knife that a classmate owned. I stopped by to see him one day and I found him gone, but his knife was on his bed. In an instant, I put the knife in my pocket. Not long after that, I was sent to sea.

After a year's cruise, I returned to the school for specialized training, and guess who was there? Things were different now, however. I had recommitted my life to Christ and wanted to please God. But I knew God would never be pleased as long as I had the knife. So I again dropped by the man's room, and again he was gone. I thought of leaving the knife, but just as I reached in my pocket, there he was. I fumbled with my words and his knife as he stared on. "Over a year ago I stole your knife. Here it is. I'm sorry." He said nothing as he took the treasure from me. "If it is not in good enough shape, I'll pay you for it," I offered. But he only thanked me for returning it.

I felt sorrow for having sinned against this man, but I felt very good for having made it right. It was indeed the right thing to do. A few months later during a special Navy birthday celebration, my ship gave out prizes from a lottery drawing. My number was pulled. Guess what I won? A Buck knife.

God, you are pleased and we are healed when we make things right.

Step Nine: Made direct amends to such people wherever possible, except when to do so would injure them or others.

Scripture: Therefore encourage one another and build each other up, just as in fact you are doing. (1 Thess. 5:11)

The following is an amends letter written to someone who really needed to be encouraged and built up. I wrote the letter to the person I had hurt the most, myself.

"Dear Jerry, I am sorry for being so angry with you that you always were frightened. I am sorry for being so negative about you and for not allowing you to forget your past mistakes. You could never feel good about yourself. I am sorry for keeping you so tense and up-tight that you still live with the pain. I regret having made you take so much strong and addictive medicine. I dulled the pain but lost life's flavor. I apologize for not taking better care of your body. You lost years of life. I am sorry for not getting you closer to God. You could have been changed long ago. I am sorry that I held you back and prevented you from having friends. You can never recapture those losses. I deeply regret the separation I put between you and your family. You have lost precious years.

"Jerry, I cannot change yesterday, but I can show my genuine regret through my change today. It is hard for me to say this next thing, and I'm not sure I believe it yet, but here goes: I love you, Jerry."

The most important amend that any of us will ever make is the amend we make to ourselves.

God of encouragement, help me face myself.

Step Nine: Made direct amends to such people wherever possible, except when to do so would injure them or others.

Scripture: Therefore stop passing judgment on one another. Instead, make up your mind not to put any stumbling block or obstacle in your brother's way. (Rom. 14:13)

Some time ago, my niece announced her intention to marry one of my best friends. I was shocked, steamed, and very self-righteous. My friend is older than my niece; he's divorced; he has children; he's behind in child support; and he's unemployed. I was filled with criticism and condemnation for the relationship. I felt it was wrong, and I was going to tell them.

Then I heard my family complain. I watched my kids treat my friend coldly and cruelly. They ignored him to his face and amplified all his negatives without any thought of his good. As I watched my family, I saw myself. I was just like them—only worse. I could hear my own damning words being spoken by my children. They learned to despise this relationship from my attitude and behavior. I had hurt my niece, my friend, and my family at the same time. I had enough trouble with my life; why should I judge others or try to control their choices? It was time to make amends.

I apologized to my kids and pointed out my failure and its influence over them. And then I faced both my niece and my friend. I explained what I had felt, done, and said. I admitted to the damage and asked for their forgiveness.

The amend kept me from losing a niece. I will lose my friend, however. But that's okay—I'll be gaining a nephew-in-law.

Just Judge, I don't want your job. Help me to quickly make amends when I've judged another.

Step Nine: Made direct amends to such people wherever possible, except when to do so would injure them or others.

Scripture: But love your enemies, do good to them, and lend to them without expecting to get anything back. Then your reward will be great, and you will be sons of the Most High, because he is kind to the ungrateful and wicked. (Luke 6:35–36)

As they approached the Iraqi bunker, the colonel instructed the two young soldiers to use caution. In an unexpected flurry, three Iraqis emerged with weapons in hand. The colonel reached for his sidearm, but his pistol was caught in his holster. "Shoot, damn it!" he screamed. But the two young men, who had already been seasoned by two days of killing, held their fire. The colonel said he would have killed all three enemy soldiers had he released his weapon, but the two young Americans were content to understand the Iraqis' intentions.

When they saw the Americans, the starved and bewildered Iraqis dropped their unloaded guns and lifted their hands. Tears filled their eyes as they cried, "No shoot. No fight."

The colonel choked as he told this story to a news crew. He said, "I've never seen more fierce warriors or more compassionate human beings than these American boys. We can all be proud."

When it comes to facing our defects and shortcomings, we need to be fierce warriors. But when it comes to dealing with people, like the ones we've harmed or the ones who have harmed us, we need to show compassion and understanding. When we do that, we are modeling God's character. God approaches his enemies with the hope of peace. We should too.

God, to hate the enemy is our way; to love the enemy is yours. May my amends bring peace.

Step Nine: Made direct amends to such people wherever possible, except when to do so would injure them or others.

Scripture: Let no debt remain outstanding, except the continuing debt to love one another, for he who loves his fellowman has fulfilled the law. (Rom. 13:8)

*T*he worship service had somehow become very mellow and emotional. The worship leader instructed everyone to go around and share the love and peace of Christ with one another. I was off to the side where I was playing an instrument when Emma approached me. The elderly woman, who was known for her criticism and gossip, looked quite serious and not at all loving. She said with all the sternness of a mean librarian, "Now I've got to get something off my chest, okay?" I gulped and nodded. "I must admit that I've said some pretty nasty things about you behind your back. You've done an awful lot of new things around here that I don't like; but still, I have no right to run you down—no matter how much you might deserve it. I apologize and I want you to forgive me. Well, what do you say?"

"I don't know what to say, Emma. I guess I. . . . Well, I mean . . . I accept your apology."

"Good," she grunted. "If you were more like our last pastor, Brother Rigormortis, God rest his soul, I wouldn't be tempted to criticize you. Still, you're young—you'll grow into the job. I just hope to live long enough to see it."

You can imagine how I felt after Emma's amend to me. She made me feel like I was the one who should be making the amend to her. Emma did do me some good, however. I learned how *not* to make an amend.

Gracious Lord, don't let my amends injure the very ones I hope to heal.

Step Nine: Made direct amends to such people wherever possible, except when to do so would injure them or others.

Scripture: Do not repay anyone evil for evil. Be careful to do what is right in the eyes of everybody. If it is possible, as far as it depends on you, live at peace with everyone. (Rom. 12:17–18)

I had rarely seen such anger in a meeting. A woman was justifying her reasons for not making amends to her ex-husband. "I may have hurt him," she growled, "but he deserved whatever he got! I'm not about to forgive or make amends to that S.O.B."

This woman was new to the program and had not yet worked Step Nine. We just happened to be discussing it that night, and it struck a very sore spot in this woman. No one sought to correct her or give advice. Everyone listened and supported her right to vent.

I didn't speak when she exploded that night, but I watched. I saw the pain that her unforgiveness created, I saw the hatred that her defiance fueled, and I saw the deep hurt that her offenses sustained. And I saw all of the same things in me. I had done Step Nine long before, but some of the feelings that this woman shared struck a sympathetic chord in me. I found feelings of unforgiveness, desires for retaliation, and memories of offenses. I wasn't thinking of her husband, of course, but the faces and names of my tormentors resurfaced. For a moment, I lost my serenity in a sea of anger. But the pain in this woman's face reminded me that those feelings are better off left with God. I can't afford to nurture an offense or retaliate. I need to make the amends and forgive.

God, help me to remember it is far healthier to live at peace with others, even with those who don't deserve it.

Step Nine: Made direct amends to such people wherever possible, except when to do so would injure them or others.

Scripture: Do nothing out of selfish ambition or vain conceit, but in humility consider others better than yourselves. Each of you should look not only to your own interests, but also to the interests of others. (Phil. 2:3–4)

My son R.J. and I escaped Grandma and Grandpa's house for a while to regain our sanity. We found ourselves down near the beach. I was concentrating on traffic when R.J. announced, "Look, Dad, there's an orphan!" I turned in time to see a very soiled and sorry-looking man heaped at the side of the street. A bulging plastic garbage bag lay between his legs, which blocked the sidewalk, and his head was propped up by a filthy sleeping bag.

"Why did you say he was an orphan, R.J.?"

"Because he looks like he has no parents," he answered.

At that moment, it would have been very easy to repeat the tired phrase, "There but for the grace of God . . ." Instead, I thought that this man was indeed an orphan so long as sanctimonious people like me judge him as a lower form of life. So I asked R.J. what he thought the man needed. R.J. said, "He needs to go to McDonald's!" So we bought a McDonald's gift certificate, and I presented it to the man in R.J.'s name.

R.J. helped me remember that day that God's grace comes through people—through caring people like R.J., who saw an orphan, not a bum. Don't be selfish with God's grace. There are orphans all around who need your concern and care.

God, show me my vain conceit and selfish pride, and help me consider others as more important.

STEP TEN

Continued to take personal inventory and, when we were wrong, promptly admitted it.

*S*o, if you think you are standing firm, be careful that you don't fall. *(1 Cor. 10:12)*

Step Ten Reflections

God views our salvation as a process, and Step Ten helps us remember that. That doesn't mean we aren't saved now. We are saved right now, but we are saved a little more each day. We are saved from ourselves: our defects and their effects. The Book of Proverbs says that God's people are like the dawning of the morning. We grow brighter and brighter until the day is full. The Apostle Paul said that he was not perfect, but he was pressing toward the mark day by day.

In Step Ten we are encouraged to keep up the process of personal inventory, to examine our lives for the good and the not so good every day. The Holy Spirit helps us take inventory and helps us admit our faults when we are wrong. Remember that none of the program is human powered. Every step is accomplished in God's strength and in God's time.

Perfection eludes us. We never stop growing, changing, and recovering. The day we believe that we have recovered is the day denial recaptures our minds and hearts. With God's help we can include the working of Step Ten (which is actually a review of Steps Four through Nine) in our daily devotional and journaling time. In this way Step Ten becomes a guide and aids us in our daily spiritual journey—a journey we have only just begun.

Step Ten: Continued to take personal inventory and, when we were wrong, promptly admitted it.

Scripture: Whoever of you loves life and desires to see many good days, keep your tongue from evil and your lips from speaking lies. Turn from evil and do good; seek peace and pursue it. (Ps. 34:12)

*O*ver the years, the stories of many of my experiences have taken on legendary proportion. I have spun more imagination than truth into some of the recollections. That's okay, I suppose, when I'm telling the kids a bedtime story, but I've noticed that I change history a bit when I talk to adults as well.

I was on jury duty recently, and during the time when the lawyers questioned us potential jurors for a trial, they began to ask me questions about my past. I was scared to death. I was under oath to tell the truth. I had to think hard with each question to make sure that my answer was the true truth and not my exaggeration. With the help of God, I told the truth. I also got picked for a trial.

This process of keeping one's self on the "straight and narrow" is what Step Ten is all about. I've realized that I need the continual inventory that Step Ten suggests. One of my many defects has been lying or exaggerating. The program helps me stay on top of my lingering defects through the daily process of taking inventory.

Tales and legends are fine when told at story time, but when we tell tales to feel better about ourselves and our past, it's wrong.

Lord, you accept me just the way I am. I don't have to lie to impress you or to feel good about myself.

Step Ten: Continued to take personal inventory and, when we were wrong, promptly admitted it.

Scripture: For by the grace given me I say to every one of you: Do not think of yourself more highly than you ought, but rather think of yourself with sober judgment, in accordance with the measure of faith God has given you. (Rom. 12:13)

Years ago at ball games in my home town, my brother Rex hung out behind the concession stand. The arm-wrestling contests back there were always more interesting than the ball games, and you could bet money on the wrestlers if you were so inclined.

Now, Rex, who was more bear than man, never lost. And he was always a good bet when somebody from another town thought they could beat him. Rex would even bet before he saw his opponent. One night that changed. Some guys bet on a kid named Terry. The name Terry didn't sound very intimidating. We could all imagine some wimpy, whiny guy showing up to challenge Rex.

We waited behind the stand when suddenly we heard a moan from the crowd. I thought it was about the ball game, but when the bleachers emptied out and the crowd came to us, we knew Terry had arrived. He was as tall as the concession stand and nearly as wide. His face was uglier than a Black Angus bull's, and his arms were like tree trunks. With thunderous voice he said, "Where's Rex?" A hundred fingers pointed to my brother, and Rex swallowed hard.

Rex's arm healed in time, and we made up the money. But Rex's ego was never the same. Like Rex, we might be tempted to think that we can handle all comers in our life, but we are still the same person who began with Step One so long ago. As long as we keep taking an honest inventory, we'll do okay.

God, I may get better, but I'll never outgrow my need to examine myself with honesty and humility.

Step Ten: *Continued to take personal inventory and, when we were wrong, promptly admitted it.*

Scripture: *Settle matters quickly with your adversary who is taking you to court. Do it while you are still with him on the way, or he may hand you over to the judge, and the judge may hand you over to the officer, and you may be thrown into prison. I tell you the truth, you will not get out until you have paid the last penny. (Matt. 5:25–26)*

"Who's been using my tools?" I angrily demanded. All eyes looked to R.J. But he acted as though he hadn't heard me. "Who left my socket set opened and on the garage floor, R.J.?"

Finally, he lifted his eyes to mine and feigned a phony smile. "I think maybe I did, Dad."

"What have I told you about my tools?" I snapped.

"Never touch Dad's tools unless you ask," he recited with exact precision.

"Then why didn't you ask? Go to your room! I'll be in later." With that R.J. stood. He walked to his room as if he were marching to death row. When I entered the room, tears already marked his cheeks, and he said, "You use my stuff and don't ask!"

"What? What have I used?" I demanded.

"Well, you slept in my bed last night, you used my tape recorder, you used my markers . . ." his list went on, and in each case, he was right. Finally he asked, "Are you gonna spank me?"

"No," I said, "but I am gonna ask you to forgive me."

Many times over, my kids have helped me in my ongoing personal inventory. Many times I've had to admit my faults and make things right after the wise counsel of my little ones.

God, you are faithful to point out my harm to others. Help me make things right.

Step Ten: Continued to take personal inventory and, when we were wrong, promptly admitted it.

Scripture: Therefore each of you must put off falsehood and speak truthfully to his neighbor, for we are all members of one body. "In your anger do not sin": Do not let the sun go down while you are still angry, and do not give the devil a foothold. He who has been stealing must steal no longer, but must work, doing something useful with his own hands, that he may have something to share with those in need. (Eph. 4:25–28)

Just after the matinee had begun, she heard the laugh. The voice was unmistakable. She remembered how that voice had been used to belittle and humiliate. Her neck and shoulders grew tense as she thought of this woman sitting behind her. "I wonder if she saw me," she thought. "I can't let her ruin my afternoon. You idiot, enjoy the movie; forget about her." But the tension never ceased and the movie lost all appeal. "Damn her for being here. I hate her."

As the movie ended she debated, "Should I sneak out the front exit or leave normally? I'll be damned if I'll let her control me anymore. I'll go out through the lobby." But as she turned to leave, there she was.

"Oh, hi, Lois! I didn't know you were behind me," she said through clenched teeth. "How are you?" The courteous yet unbearable conversation lasted only a moment, but the effect lingered. She pounded the steering wheel, "Why was I nice to her? I should have told her what a witch she is and how she ruined my life. So much for my nice afternoon off."

Both friends and enemies will pop into our lives from time to time. Their appearances may be welcome or painful reminders. In either event, let them help you keep inventory on how you're doing.

God, you know what I'll face in my life today. Please prepare me to make the right choices.

Step Ten: Continued to take personal inventory and, when we were wrong, promptly admitted it.

Scripture: Anyone who listens to the word but does not do what it says is like a man who looks at his face in a mirror and, after looking at himself, goes away and immediately forgets what he looks like. But the man who looks intently into the perfect law that gives freedom, and continues to do this, not forgetting what he has heard, but doing it—he will be blessed in what he does. (James 1:23–25)

On my bookshelf among great texts and lofty works is the little catechism book I used as a child. It contains the great truths and confessions of the Church, and it contains my juvenile comments and handwriting. I keep it as a reminder.

The little catechism reminds me that the truths of God's Word and the tenets of God's Church are never changing. They endure through time and testing. But the little catechism also reminds me of my life. The scribbled handwriting and youthful comments, which mark the book and date it in my life, remind me that I have changed.

That's the way it is with God in the program. God's Word and the principles of the Twelve Steps are unchanging, but we are not. We grow and develop as we measure and examine ourselves in God's Word and in the truths of the Twelve Steps.

I've changed in my faith over the years and that little catechism will always be a testimony to my growth. Our Step Four inventory is a testimony to our growth. Look at it often and remember, but also remember that, as Step Ten says, the process of accessing our progress is ongoing and daily.

Righteous God, your Word is a standard in my life. Help me measure myself by it daily.

Step Ten: *Continued to take personal inventory and, when we were wrong, promptly admitted it.*

Scripture: *Therefore, if anyone is in Christ, he is a new creation; the old has gone, the new has come! (2 Cor. 5:17)*

Snowflake is forever under Norm's feet. When he sits down, she is right there playfully nudging his hands with her wet nose or lovingly licking him. "Pet me. Don't you know I love you, Norm?" she seems to say.

"My daughter actually found Snowflake," reported Norm. "She rushed in the house all out of breath yelling, 'Come help, Dad! A dog's been hit!' I went out to find a little dog laying bloody and broken in the street. Although she couldn't get up, her tail tried to wag as she saw me. I scooped her up and headed to the vet, but the vet said we should put her to sleep. Her pelvis was damaged, back leg broken, and she was bleeding inside. But I couldn't put her to sleep. I didn't even know who she belonged to, but I told the vet to keep her overnight. I found the owner that night, he had nine other pups and said he couldn't afford a sick one. 'Put her to sleep,' he said. But I couldn't.

"God must have loved that pup a lot because she made it through that night and on to a full recovery." Norm was embarrassed by his tears, but he added, "I love that crazy dog, and I think she loves me." That was an understatement.

We who are in recovery are becoming new creations because of God's healing love and compassion. We were bloodied and broken, but Christ has redeemed us. Use Step Ten to keep the healing going.

Caring Master, you wanted me when all others had given up. Thank you for your love.

Step Ten: Continued to take personal inventory and, when we were wrong, promptly admitted it.

Scripture: You were taught, with regard to your former way of life, to put off your old self, which is being corrupted by its deceitful desire; to be made new in the attitude of your minds; and to put on the new self, created to be like God in true righteousness and holiness. (Eph. 4:22–24)

Although she had changed a lot, few of her old friends wanted to be around her. They would talk among themselves and say how they hated to ask her how she was. One said, "If I'd ask her how she was, I'd cringe and think 'What will her problem be today?' Either she complained about her poor health or her awful husband. She whined about how poor they were or what bad luck they seemed to have. She always made me feel sorry for them or guilty for having a better life than her. I just can't stand to be around her." The others would always agree or add their particular story about her.

Some of us have been like this woman. We have abused our friends and manipulated them in order to elicit sympathy or support. And although we may have been in recovery for some time, those former ways linger. We must be ever vigilant to "put off the old self." We have a new life and new ways—God's life and God's ways.

New friends will come in time. They will be attracted by the new life growing within us. And they will be our friends, not because we have manipulated them, but because they see us for who we really are and value us.

God, you have changed me and made me new. Please never let me stop growing.

Step Ten: Continued to take personal inventory and, when we were wrong, promptly admitted it.

Scripture: A patient man has great understanding, but a quick-tempered man displays folly. A heart at peace gives life to the body, but envy rots the bones. (Prov. 14:29–30)

She hated summer. To her, summer meant that her kids would be home from school invading her life, her time, her space, and her sanity. Past summers were cruel memories of screaming threats, angry fights, struggling strong wills, fatigue, exhaustion, and hard work. As an adult child she fought with her kids as if they were rivals. But this summer was different. She was in recovery and understood that her children needed positive direction, not angry discipline.

She had planned activities, enrolled the kids in the library's book club, signed everyone up for swimming lessons. She had even planned to swap baby-sitting times with a friend so that she could have some alone time to regain her sanity. Things weren't perfect, but they were very different. Even the kids noticed the change in her and in the house. Peace replaced pandemonium, and serenity replaced strife.

The composure and peace, which the program gives us, empowers us to overcome even our worst nightmares. And more—when we are at peace, it is easier to think of others and to consider their needs.

We can use Step Ten to keep watch over our serenity and to police our treatment of others.

Watchful Lord, help me jealously guard the advances I've made.

Step Ten: Continued to take personal inventory and, when we were wrong, promptly admitted it.

Scripture: So, if you think you are standing firm, be careful that you don't fall. (1 Cor. 10:12)

I am very fortunate to have a beautiful solid oak desk. It was given to me nearly four years ago by a friend who wanted a "man of God" to have it. I guess he couldn't find one; he gave it to me. I see the desk every day, and when I see it, I remember a significant defect in my life.

The bottom left drawer of my desk is slightly cockeyed due to a certain little boy's horseplay. When the drawer was fully extended one day, R.J. sat on it. The supports and guides broke and so did I. I really lost it, and I severely disciplined R.J. out of anger. My wife moderated the anger, and my apology to R.J. was more necessary than his apology to me. My anger that day frightened me. I wasn't frightened that I might physically hurt R.J.; I never would, but I was afraid that the picture R.J. would remember of me would be one of an angry and unmerciful dad.

Somehow we all got beyond that day. I repaired the desk but was never able to make it exactly right. The cockeyed drawer will always remind me, not of R.J.'s actions, but of my anger. The drawer will forever serve as a warning for me to be on guard.

We must all be careful of overconfidence. Our defects and flaws are healed only to the degree that we recognize them and submit them to God's power.

Help me remember, God, that I'm not perfect. You alone are without defect or blemish.

Step Ten: Continued to take personal inventory and, when we were wrong, promptly admitted it.

Scripture: Be very careful, then, how you live—not as unwise but as wise, making the most of every opportunity, because the days are evil. (Eph. 5:15-16)

I had slipped into the testimony service for some moral support since there were no Twelve-Step meetings available. Three sweet older folks stood and thanked God for their salvation. God had saved one woman over fifty-six years earlier. She and the congregation praised God for his goodness in her life over half a century before. The two others had similar testimonies, and the crowd reacted in the same approving way.

Then in the back, a rather dark character stood. His hair was matted, his clothes were wrinkled, his manner was jittery and nervous. He began to apologize for his appearance, and he covered his mouth to hide his missing teeth. "I guess I shouldn't even stand up in this place 'cause I'm a stranger. But I'm no stranger to God. I wanta thank God for keepin' me safe today. Today I ain't used, and I ain't drunk nothin' today. Well, I guess I just wanta thank God. Sorry." The crowd didn't react; they didn't applaud his testimony; they didn't give God any glory. They only stared for a moment, then looked back to the platform. The interruption was over.

Of all the testimonies I heard that night, that man's was the best because it was about today. I care about today. I made my decision to follow Christ today. I made a choice to follow the program today. I thank God for his help yesterday, but I want his salvation today.

God, your Word says today is the day of salvation.

STEP ELEVEN

Sought through prayer and meditation to improve our conscious contact with God as we understood him, praying only for knowledge of his will for us and the power to carry that out.

*L*et the word of Christ dwell in you richly. *(Col. 3:16a)*

Step Eleven Reflections

*H*igher Power is more than a concept and more than a force. Our Higher Power is a personal and loving God who wants close intimate fellowship with his people. Step Eleven encourages that fellowship and contact. When the rest of the world was worshiping the stars, God was among his people. During the Exodus, God was present in the cloud covering his people by day. At night he was present in a pillar of fire keeping them warm. His tabernacle was always among them, and his presence was always near. The people didn't need to seek things. They just stayed near God. His presence met their needs for food, water, and protection.

In the New Testament time, God drew near us in Christ—Emmanuel, "God with us." He showed himself again to be a God who wants close contact with his people. And now, today, God comes by his Holy Spirit right into our hearts and lives. He lives within us. We can access his presence in our lives through prayer and meditation. He will instruct us from within and empower us to live lives pleasing to him. He will teach us from his Word and direct us according to his will. He only asks that we take the time to know him, to hear him, to honor him, and to draw near him.

Prayer is foreign to many of us. We may know prayers, but we don't know how to pray. We need to remember that God is a person, and prayer ought to be communication similar to conversation with another person. God longs to hear our petitions and praises, our complaints and confessions, and our invocations and invectives. He wants it all.

God also longs to see us step aside from life's fast pace for the purpose of meditation. He has much to offer us if we are willing and quiet enough to listen. The most important of God's offerings to us is the knowledge of his will for us.

Step Eleven: Sought through prayer and meditation to improve our conscious contact with God as we understood him, praying only for knowledge of his will for us and the power to carry that out.

Scripture: The good man brings good things out of the good stored up in his heart. For out of outflow of his heart his mouth speaks. (Luke 6:45)

*R*ecently, I attended the early service alone. I sat next to a woman I didn't know. She sang with great confidence and volume. Although I didn't try to match her, I also belted out the hymns in my regular fashion. When the service was done, we waited to be dismissed by the ushers. The woman began to stir and inch toward me. "You have a beautiful voice," she said. "Would you consider joining the choir?"

Now in the past, when someone talked to me like that, I resisted any conversation and rebutted any compliments. But I surprised myself when I answered, "Thank you. I'm afraid the choir wouldn't fit my schedule right now. Are you in the choir?"

"No, I just thought your voice belonged there. Are you a regular attender?" And so the conversation went on.

You may be wondering why all this is significant. But just the fact that I responded in a friendly and talkative way to this woman was a miracle. I've been so hurt by people in recent years that I have become sort of a social hermit. My simple yet cordial response was an indication to me that some recovery and change had begun to take place in my heart. God has had my heart "under reconstruction" for the last few years, and I'm beginning to see the new improvements. God's will for me is to be friendly and to engage people. What is he doing in your life?

Thanks, Lord, for the work you've been doing in my life. Keep it up.

Step Eleven: Sought through prayer and meditation to improve our conscious contact with God as we understood him, praying only for knowledge of his will for us and the power to carry that out.

Scripture: Therefore I tell you, whatever you ask for in prayer, believe that you have received it, and it will be yours. And when you stand praying, if you hold anything against anyone, forgive him, so that your Father in heaven may forgive you your sins. (Mark 11:24)

*L*ate last night I dropped off two important letters at the post office. Although it was nearly ten o'clock, there was still a man sitting out front with a cardboard sign. I ignored him on the way in to the building, but I stopped and read his sign on the way out. It read, "Will work for food."

The letters I dropped off were copies of my résumé. I was applying for work in a new career. But somehow that man and his sign frightened me. I could see myself sitting there. And the voice in my head said, "You stupid, what makes you think that you can apply for those jobs? You're the last one they'd pick. You'd better just go back to doing what you've always done. Quit whining and make the best of it."

Many codependents like me stay in careers that are not really fulfilling to us or healthy for us. We enter careers that we are not suited for in order to make others happy, and we get stuck in those jobs because we are frightened to leave. We fulfill the desires of others and ignore our own.

After I saw that man and dropped off the mail, I told God about my fear. Although I didn't feel anything emotionally, I just had faith that God wants me to be happy in what I do. I choose to believe that God will help me find fulfillment in a career that I want.

You want what is best for me, Lord. Give me faith to believe in your goodness and not my fear.

Step Eleven: Sought through prayer and meditation to improve our conscious contact with God as we understood him, praying only for knowledge of his will for us and the power to carry that out.

Scripture: Let us acknowledge the Lord; let us press on to acknowledge him. As surely as the sun rises, he will appear; he will come to us like the winter rains, like the spring rains that water the earth. (Hos. 6:3)

With a cup of her favorite herbal tea in hand, she settled into her chair. Her Bible, journal, and devotional book were all waiting, and she had just enough time to do a good morning devotion. But just after she opened the devotion to the right page, she remembered that she didn't put honey in her tea. She got up for the honey, but on her way back she remembered an important call she needed to make later in the day. So she went to her date book to make a note. As she opened the date book, her attention was captured by her busy agenda for the day. She settled in again only to realize that she was hurriedly skimming the day's devotional, not savoring or meditating. She felt her pulse quickening as she mentally rehearsed a conversation she would have later in the day and as she thought of all she had to accomplish. Suddenly the Bible didn't seem important. The day was getting away from her. She had to go. The tea was not touched. The honey sat unused. The Bible left unopened.

The time we spend with God is not wasted or unimportant. The time we spend with God in the morning is foundational for the success of our day. Martin Luther once said that he had so much to do one day that he needed to pray three hours instead of one. When we spend time in prayer and meditation, the work is easier, the day is smoother, and the results are better.

God, help me remember that I can't afford to miss my time with you. You're my most important appointment.

Step Eleven: Sought through prayer and meditation to improve our conscious contact with God as we understood him, praying only for knowledge of his will for us and the power to carry that out.

Scripture: But when you pray, go into your room, close the door and pray to your Father, who is unseen. Then your Father, who sees what is done in secret, will reward you. (Matt. 6:6)

My prayer room is about thirty-five or forty acres in size and carpeted with beautiful green grass. Some people would call my prayer room a city park, but what's in a name? I enter my place of prayer quite early, while the dew is still on the ground. Usually my only company is a stray dog. For him the park is not a place of prayer.

I circle the park on foot, and I talk to God. I begin by thanking him. Then, following a prayerful assessment of the day before, I usually confess my sins and defects. I follow confession with complaint. I tell God everything that bothers me. God hears my protest about world problems and personal predicaments. Then he hears my petitions—prayer for me and others. I conclude by quoting the Twelve Steps and the Serenity Prayer. And, if I'm in the mood, I season the whole time with singing. The stray dog loves this part the best.

Someone once said, "He who has no regular time and place for prayer does not pray." I know that's right. Make a daily appointment with God. Meet him at the same time and place every day. Don't squeeze God in. Give him your best, not the leftovers.

Thanks for meeting me again today, God. See ya tomorrow, same time, same place.

***Step Eleven: Sought through prayer and meditation to improve
our conscious contact with God as we understood him, praying
only for knowledge of his will for us and the power to carry
that out.***

Scripture: *Show me your ways, O Lord, teach me your paths; guide me
in your truth and teach me, for you are God my Savior, and my hope
is in you all day long. (Ps. 25:4–5)*

*F*rom the day he met Christ during the
Jesus Movement of the Sixties, Bobby Mallory knew he was
called to Ecuador. He bought a one-way ticket and was miraculously allowed to enter the country. He hiked three days toward a
remote mountain range where people had never heard of Christ.
But an army patrol found him near death, shot by poison darts.
After medical care, he started again. But his right arm was forever paralyzed. After three days he approached a village where
men beat him with clubs and crushed his right eye. The army
was nearer this time and saved his life. But after a short stay in
the hospital he went again. Half paralyzed and half blind he went
to fulfill God's call. The army accompanied him this time and
even interpreted for him. The army interpreter became his first
convert.

Four years later, Bible translators came to that same mountain range. They found over twenty vibrant churches, all started
by Bobby. They also found Bobby. He was buried in a shallow
grave. This giant died of TB at the age of twenty.

God is looking for people who will say yes to his will.
Sacrifice is possible, but satisfaction and success are guaranteed.

***Show me your ways, O Lord, teach me your paths. I'll follow
so long as you lead the way.***

Step Eleven: Sought through prayer and meditation to improve our conscious contact with God as we understood him, praying only for knowledge of his will for us and the power to carry that out.

Scripture: Ask and it will be given to you; seek and you will find; knock and the door will be opened to you. (Matt. 7:7)

We were walking around the parking lot outside of Kay's quarters on the Navy base. My heart was pounding as I considered telling her what was on my mind. I remembered the passage in Proverbs that says, "Open rebuke is better than secret love." So I decided to tell her. "I love you, Kay!" I blurted out. But silence came back. The only sound was the crackling of eucalyptus leaves under our feet. "Well?" I asked.

"Well," she answered, "I do love you, I love you like a brother, a Christian brother."

After she picked me up from the ground, I asked, "Does that mean you don't want to see me anymore?"

"I still want to see you."

"Is there hope?" I pried.

"There's always hope," she said with a smile. And, in time, that hope turned into real love and a lasting relationship.

Our fellowship with God is very much like this. God wants to be known and sought after. I believe God's heart is pained when we see him as some Celestial Santa Claus who is there to dispense blessings and answers to prayers. God is a person, the creator of love. When we ask for *him*, seek for *him*, and knock for *him*, he will be found. And when he is found, he freely shares his blessing, his goodness, and the knowledge of his will for us.

Heavenly Father, I want to seek you for who you are, and not for what you can do for me.

Step Eleven: Sought through prayer and meditation to improve our conscious contact with God as we understood him, praying only for knowledge of his will for us and the power to carry that out.

Scripture: Blessed is the man who does not walk in the counsel of the wicked or stand in the way of sinners or sit in the seat of mockers. But his delight is in the law of the Lord, and on his law he meditates day and night. He is like a tree planted by streams of water, which yields its fruit in season and whose leaf does not wither. Whatever it does prospers. (Ps. 1:1–3)

Sissy is a wonderful Christian lady with the best of intentions, but she is also an amateur spiritualist. If you're with her any amount of time, she will want to study your palm, decipher your tea leaves, or read your cards. She has even been known to consult the dead. Although her intentions are always the very best, her methods raise more than a few eyebrows.

Like Sissy, many of us have some old ways that want to follow us into our new lives. But the old standards by which we judged and measured life are out of date in Christ. We don't do things because they feel right or because "we've always done it that way." In Christ, we do things according to God's plan as set forth in his instruction manual, the Bible.

As we read and meditate in God's Word, we will see and understand how God wants his people to operate. We will see sinful men and women who lived and learned under God's direction. And we will see how things are done in God's kingdom.

Extend a hand to Sissy, and she'll read your palm. Extend a hand to God, and he'll lead you in his ways.

Here is my hand, Lord, lead me to the fruitfulness and prosperity of your Word.

Step Eleven: Sought through prayer and meditation to improve our conscious contact with God as we understood him, praying only for knowledge of his will for us and the power to carry that out.

Scripture: Your word is a lamp to my feet and a light for my path. I have taken an oath and confirmed it, that I will follow your righteous laws. (Ps. 119:105–106)

*I*t was early Monday morning, and I had to travel south for a business meeting. I got behind a large truck carrying steel, and I decided to follow close behind him. We were clipping along about seventy miles an hour when I remembered the sermon the day before. The pastor said, "How can you expect to get to first base in God's kingdom when you don't even obey the laws of man?"

"Oops!" I thought. "I'd better slow down and begin to obey the state and God." I slowed to fifty-five and fell far behind the truck. Suddenly I hit a thick patch of fog as I headed up a hill. With only seconds to react, I swerved to miss a pile of steel in the middle of the freeway. The truck I had been following had lost its load. Had I been closely following that truck when the load dropped, I would have been killed. Obeying God's appointed authority that day saved my life.

I've learned to test my commitment to God's Law by seeing how well I obey man's. God has made his will clear for us, and it is not always in the Bible. Sometimes his word is "55 MPH" or "stop." Obedience is not always easy, but it could save your life as well as your soul.

God, help me learn obedience in the simple things so that I might not fail the larger tests.

Step Eleven: *Sought through prayer and meditation to improve our conscious contact with God as we understood him, praying only for knowledge of his will for us and the power to carry that out.*

Scripture: *Do not be anxious about anything, but in everything, by prayer and petition, with thanksgiving, present your requests to God. (Phil. 4:6)*

We needn't ever be afraid to be honest with God in prayer. Honesty marks the Negro spirituals as genuine.

> Didn't my Lord deliver Daniel,
> didn't my Lord deliver Daniel,
> And why not every man?
> He delivered Daniel from the lion's den,
> Jonah from the belly of the whale,
> And the Hebrew children from the fiery furnace,
> And why not every man?

This Negro spiritual asks the hard question. If God delivered Daniel, Jonah, and the Hebrew children, what about me? "Here I am in trouble and hurting, Lord. Help me?"

King David of Israel took his anxieties, concerns, and complaints to the Lord. In Psalm 44 he said, "Awake, O Lord! Why do you sleep? Rouse yourself! Do not reject us forever. Why do you hide your face and forget our misery and oppression?"

My prayers are more like, "Hey God! Where am I gonna get the money for rent? What about my health insurance? What about that stupid car? I can't afford to fix it, I can't afford to buy a new one, and I can't afford to keep it! Are you listening, Lord?"

It's okay to be honest with God. He can handle it, and he alone can help.

Lord, didn't you deliver Daniel, Jonah, and the Hebrew children? What about me?

Step Eleven: Sought through prayer and meditation to improve our conscious contact with God as we understood him, praying only for knowledge of his will for us and the power to carry that out.

Scripture: If you believe, you will receive whatever you ask for in prayer. (Matt. 21:22)

I had renewed my commitment to Christ and I was riding high. My ship was in the Gulf of Tonkin off of Vietnam, the ship's store was out of toothpaste and so was I. Simple thing, right? Well, I knew that God cared even about clean teeth. So as I laid in my rack that night I prayed, "God, you know I need toothpaste and you know that nobody has any, but I know that you can help. Please give me some toothpaste. Amen." I knew it was settled. Somehow God would provide for my need.

I slept in the next morning because I had been on a late watch. When I entered the shower it was a mess. Everyone had come and gone an hour before. Wrappers, papers, and old razors cluttered the sinks, but there in pristine condition was a tiny sample of Pepsodent toothpaste! "The heavens be praised!" I cried aloud. I lifted both hands to heaven, I closed my eyes, and I began to sing the Hallelujah chorus. When I reemerged from my worshipful trance, I saw two bewildered sailors watching me. I showed them both the tiny tube of toothpaste and said, "God just gave me this tube!" I'm sure they thought I had been at sea too long.

God delights in answering the prayers of his people. Nothing is too insignificant. The Bible says he knows the number of hairs on our heads. But the comb is another story.

Thank you, Lord, for hearing my prayers, even the little ones.

Step Eleven: Sought through prayer and meditation to improve our conscious contact with God as we understood him, praying only for knowledge of his will for us and the power to carry that out.

Scripture: But the one who hears my words and does not put them into practice is like a man who built a house on the ground without a foundation. The moment the torrent struck that house, it collapsed and its destruction was complete. (Luke 6:49)

On March 4, 1970, at 8:55 A.M. the Woodworths' doorbell rang. An Army officer had news about their son Larry, who was to have come home that very day. "As your son's transport took off, a small missile was fired by the Vietcong from a makeshift launcher that they had erected in the night. I'm afraid no one survived."

The officer then went next door to the Dunns' and shared the identical story regarding their son Robert, who had entered the Army with Larry on the "Buddy Plan." Both families lost their only son, but the families reacted differently.

During the year that followed, the Dunns, who were filled with anger and bitterness, found it impossible to live together; they divorced. Alcohol became Mr. Dunn's anesthetic. And Mrs. Dunn turned Robert's unused room into a shrine.

The Woodworths had the same pain, cried the same tears, yet there was a difference. Larry's mom and dad grew closer, they accepted the support of their church, and they went on with life. What was the difference? One family was built on a strong foundation: Jesus Christ and his Word. One was not.

In this life we will have trouble. That's a promise. But in Christ we can face those troubles with hope.

When storms come, dear Jesus, let me hold tight to you.

Step Eleven: Sought through prayer and meditation to improve our conscious contact with God as we understood him, praying only for knowledge of his will for us and the power to carry that out.

Scripture: Whether you turn to the right or to the left, your ears will hear a voice behind you, saying, "This is the way; walk in it." (Isa. 30:21)

Sam and I were excited to be on ship in Pearl Harbor. On one of our first liberty days we decided to go to Sandy Beach, which is famous for bodysurfing in Hawaii.

We put our clothes, valuables, and glasses in a locker and blindly headed for the water. We were confused to see such a large crowd on the sand but so few people in the water. We squinted to see and understand, but nothing was apparent. So we entered the water. We had no sooner gotten wet when an announcement came over a blaring loudspeaker. "Will you two sailors get out of the water? We are trying to hold a bodysurfing contest here!"

When we finally recovered our glasses and our self-respect, we saw the ABC television cameras, the judges, and the spectators. Oops!

Like the voice over the loudspeaker, God will instruct us in the way we should walk. I often hear people say that God speaks in a still small voice, but I hear him loud and clear most of the time. He uses my wife, my kids, my friends, my mistakes, and my Bible to get his message across. I don't always obey, but I do hear him.

When God points out his way to us, we needn't be embarrassed. We can just thank him for helping us see life a little more clearly.

God, you see things more clearly than I do. I'll listen for your voice and trust your direction.

STEP TWELVE

Having had a spiritual awakening as the result of these steps, we tried to carry this message to others, and to practice these principles in all our affairs.

*B*rothers, if someone is caught in a sin, you who are spiritual should restore him gently. But watch yourselves, or you may also be tempted. *(Gal. 6:1)*

Step Twelve Reflections

*P*eople are God's number one priority. And like any father, God has always delighted in showing off his people. God wants his people to be more than just devoted followers. He wants his people to be a living demonstration to the world. God's kingdom is on display wherever obedient Christians live.

In the Old Testament, God told his people that they were a chosen and unique people who were to show forth God's power and praise. However, they failed to keep God's laws and his ways. Because of their disobedience, God's kingdom could not be seen. So Jesus came, living the perfectly obedient life and demonstrating God's kingdom flawlessly. But Jesus could not reach the whole world by himself. So he sent the Holy Spirit, who enabled the church to obey God's Word, to do God's work, and to demonstrate God's kingdom. We Christians are the light of the world, the salt to season the nations, and the hope of mankind.

The Twelve Steps are powerful biblical principles encapsulating submission, confession, repentance, obedience, redemption, evangelism, and much more into just twelve steps. The person who lives the Twelve Steps demonstrates God's kingdom in action. And that's what Step Twelve is about: living in God's kingdom's principles, sharing the program, and practicing the program in all we do.

Step Twelve, like Steps Ten and Eleven, is an ongoing process. It is the step that ensures that we don't lose touch with the power of the Steps in our daily living. Step Twelve reminds us that the program is valuable for more than just recovery issues; it is a way of life that applies to all our affairs.

Step Twelve: Having had a spiritual awakening as the result of these steps, we tried to carry this message to others, and to practice these principles in all our affairs.

Scripture: Finally, brothers, whatever is true, whatever is noble, whatever is right, whatever is pure, whatever is lovely, whatever is admirable—if anything is excellent or praiseworthy—think about such things. Whatever you have learned or received or heard from me, or seen in me—put it into practice. And the God of peace will be with you. (Phil. 4:8–9)

*T*he new dog my sister got for the farm wasn't working out. Although Sheppy was a herder by breed, he was a loafer by deed. He didn't bark at strangers. He didn't greet cars coming in the drive. And he didn't chase cattle. All he could do was eat and sleep. So Sis decided to get another dog. This time they got an Australian sheepdog named Max.

Max was great. He did it all. He barked, herded, guarded, fetched, and played. Everyone called him "Max the Wonder Dog." Everybody loved him, everybody except Sheppy. But for the first time in his life, Sheppy began to show signs of life. He began by nipping at Max's ears. He began to accompany Max around the barnyard and pastures. He kept his eyes on Max. Then one day, Sheppy began to act like Max. He started chasing cattle, barking at strangers, and playing with my nephew. Now, thanks to Max, my sister has two farm dogs.

Brian G. did that for me. When Brian introduced me to the program and opened his life, I saw the way it was supposed to be. He knew God in a very special way, and he had a peacefulness that could be felt. By watching Brian, I learned more than a program, I learned a new way of life.

Thank you, Lord, for Brian G. Give me the courage to share the program too.

Step Twelve: Having had a spiritual awakening as the result of these steps, we tried to carry this message to others, and to practice these principles in all our affairs.

Scripture: Be wise in the way you act toward outsiders; make the most of every opportunity. Let your conversation be always full of grace, seasoned with salt, so that you may know how to answer everyone. (Col. 4:5-6)

I heard about a mental patient who always looked behind himself. He would point and say, "They're following me. They're watching me. Look!" It's not just paranoia or imagination for those of us who have been in the program for a while. People are following and watching us. As the new ones sit in our meetings, they look to us for cues. They see our supportive gestures and ways. They notice how we dispense acceptance and not advice. They are put at ease when they see how we willingly share our own struggles and how we don't judge theirs.

But more than just the newcomers are watching us. Our churches, our friends, and our families are watching and following us. We must be sure that we carry the lessons of the program beyond the walls of our meetings. The spiritual lessons that the Twelve Steps teach are applicable to more than just recovery. The Twelve Steps are a way of life for anyone.

Go ahead, turn around and look. Somebody is watching you. What will they see?

Thank you for the Twelve Steps, Lord, help me to live the principles and demonstrate their effectiveness.

Step Twelve: Having had a spiritual awakening as the result of these steps, we tried to carry this message to others, and to practice these principles in all our affairs.

Scripture: Jesus did not let him, but said, "Go home to your family and tell them how much the Lord has done for you, and how he has had mercy on you." (Mark 5:19)

*T*he loss of everything dear to him made Chris face his addictive/compulsive behavior. After two years in the program, he began to feel that he was recovered, although anyone could see that he had a long way to go. He was venturing into business again, but he used the old tools of manipulation and control to get things done. So much still needed to be settled.

One night Chris's eighteen-year-old son attended a meeting with him. Chris's son had been badly damaged by Chris's behavior over the years. The boy needed the program as much as his father did, but Chris made light of his son's needs. A few of the attenders shared about the abuse they experienced as children. I could tell that Chris's son was relating to the others' experiences. But just as the boy seemed about to share, Chris butted in about his father. He blamed his father for all the pain in his life and said, "But I'm a much better dad than my father ever was. Don't you think, Son?" All eyes then turned to the son, but he hung his head and said nothing.

Many of us who are in recovery have damaged our families through our addictive/compulsive behavior, and the first place we need to share the hope of the Twelve Steps is in our own homes. Our denial and pain may keep us from admitting it, but our families need what we have to share.

Forgive me, Lord, for ignoring the need in my own family. The program can work for them too.

Step Twelve: Having had a spiritual awakening as the result of these steps, we tried to carry this message to others, and to practice these principles in all our affairs.

Scripture: Preach the word; be prepared in season and out of season; correct, rebuke and encourage—with great patience and careful instruction. (2 Tim. 4:2)

Sandy is easy to spot at a party. She is louder than anyone else and has a comment about everything. She criticizes everyone but always behind their backs. She never talks to anyone very long, but everyone feels her presence. Stan, on the other hand, is hard to spot at a party. He usually finds a comfortable spot and stays there. He hopes that he can blend into the scenery and pass the time relatively undisturbed. And he can't be counted on to keep a conversation going. Sandy and Stan appear outwardly different, but inside they're very much alike.

If there is such a thing as a universal problem with those of us in recovery, it is a problem related to our self-esteem. The one who quietly suffers as the apparent wallflower and the one who hides behind bravado and pride are the same inside. They find it difficult to accept or like themselves, but they have learned to survive. Surviving may mean hiding, pretending, running, or numbing. Healthy or not, they cope.

I believe that the most important message for us to share with adult children, codependents, addictive/compulsives, and others is the message of acceptance and grace. They need to know that God loves them and we accept them right where they are now. Help them understand that they don't have to be great, beautiful, funny, loud, or invisible for us to care.

Lord, you loved me when I was yet in my sin. Help me to tell others that they are acceptable and loved.

Step Twelve: Having had a spiritual awakening as the result of these steps, we tried to carry this message to others, and to practice these principles in all our affairs.

Scripture: Be imitators of God, therefore, as dearly loved children and live a life of love, just as Christ loved us and gave himself up for us as a fragrant offering and sacrifice. (Eph. 5:1–2)

Greg took some college kids on a hike. The group stopped to rest, but two guys rushed ahead to the sound of water. The group had only been resting for a moment when they heard an awful cry. Greg found one of the boys caught in a mighty whirlpool. Before he could decide what to do, one of the others had jumped in. The rescuer's plunge was enough to push the victim out of the whirlpool's grasp, but the rescuer himself was captured by the undertow. Everyone watched as he struggled, tired, and fell victim to the powerful force. They attached a rope to another brave soul, but he was already too deep.

When the sheriff's trained rescuers arrived, the boy had been on the bottom for thirty minutes. The force of the whirlpool made it nearly impossible even for the experts to pull his body up.

Greg later said, "That kid never thought about himself. He jumped in to save a friend and sacrificed his own life."

Remember what God's love does. It considers others more important, and it sacrifices even to the point of death. God so loved us that he gave his only Son. Jesus gladly jumped in after us. He saved us from sin's grasp. But he was caught. He struggled and then he died—all for us. Do we really want to be like God? I hope so.

Thank you, Jesus, for your sacrifice. Give me the courage and love to imitate you.

Step Twelve: Having had a spiritual awakening as the result of these steps, we tried to carry this message to others, and to practice these principles in all our affairs.

Scripture: If anyone speaks, he should do it as one speaking the very words of God. If anyone serves, he should do it with the strength God provides, so that in all things God may be praised through Jesus Christ. To him be the glory and the power forever and ever. Amen. (1 Pet. 4:11)

*I*t is said that one day a cowardly soldier was brought before Alexander the Great for judgment. When the soldier who had retreated and hidden in the face of battle stood before Alexander, the great general asked, "What is your name?"

The humiliated man lifted his eyes. "Alexander."

"What? What did you say? What is your name?" demanded the mighty conqueror.

"My name is Alexander," answered the man.

"Well then, Alexander, hear my judgment. You shall either change your character or you shall change your name." And with that the soldier was dismissed to return to the battle.

As Christians, we represent Christ and we bear his name. But more, we inherit his strength. And in his strength, we can do more than practice the Twelve Steps; we can become like him. The Spirit of God enables us to grow in God's character. We Christians, whatever our stripe, are the body of Christ. By the Holy Spirit we are Christ's hands, his feet, his mouth, and his heart.

Don't worry. We won't have to change our name *or* our character. That's God's job.

Spirit of God, make me a worthy tool for the Master's service.

Step Twelve: Having had a spiritual awakening as the result of these steps, we tried to carry this message to others, and to practice these principles in all our affairs.

Scripture: Brothers, if someone is caught in a sin, you who are spiritual should restore him gently. But watch yourselves, or you may also be tempted. (Gal. 6:1)

Most of the ladies in the group were chatting about their homes, families, husbands, and so on. All but one were talking, and she was noticeably quiet. Suddenly she bolted. Her friend followed. "What's wrong, Hon?" she asked.

"I don't belong with these women," she cried. "They're so much better. They have so much more. And their lives are together. Who am I? What can I talk about?"

Honey's friend knew her well. Honey was raised by a brutal, alcoholic father, and she grew up only to marry a man just like her dad. Honey had very little in life, and what life she had revolved around taking care of her husband and trying to survive.

"Hon, I want you to come back in. Those ladies haven't judged you. You have harshly and wrongly judged yourself. You have a lot to share with us. You need to see yourself apart from your husband. You're special, not because you take care of somebody or because you're a martyr. You're a beautiful Christian lady with a lot of love and compassion. Share that with us, Hon. Okay?"

"Wait 'til my eyes dry," Honey answered.

"No, come now. Tears are nothing to be ashamed of."

Honey's friend didn't need special insight to know Honey was judging herself harshly. But she did need special willingness to run after Honey and help her. Be willing to help.

Lord, when I blow it, send a caring friend to help me.

Step Twelve: Having had a spiritual awakening as the result of these steps, we tried to carry this message to others, and to practice these principles in all our affairs.

Scripture: Two are better than one, because they have a good return for their work: If one falls down, his friend can help him up. But pity the man who falls and has no one to help him up! Also, if two lie down together, they will keep warm. But how can one keep warm alone? (Eccles. 4:9–11)

After Brian G. had come to our church and made such a powerful impact on my life, I asked for his help in starting a Christ-centered Twelve-Step meeting. He agreed. So with the help of a few other program veterans he had brought to the church, we began. The first thing we did was to announce the meeting from the pulpit. Nobody came. So the next thing we did was to read the list of "Common Behavior Characteristics of Adult Children." (See *The Twelve Steps—A Spiritual Journey,* page 159.) We read it from the pulpit on a Sunday morning. The next meeting was packed.

People from all sorts of backgrounds and from all sorts of dysfunction saw themselves in that list of common characteristics. But the exciting thing was the change in people's lives because of the Twelve Steps and the meetings. One man, who had been estranged from his parents and siblings for twenty-five years, made things right and flew home for a visit. One woman, who could not find or keep a fulfilling job, was forever changed.

These people's lives would never have been touched had it not been for Brian G. and Heidi H. and the few others who covenanted together to start the Christ-centered meeting at the church. Don't be afraid to start something.

Thank you, Lord, for the wonderful people who so changed my life. Help me pass it on.

Step Twelve: Having had a spiritual awakening as the result of these steps, we tried to carry this message to others, and to practice these principles in all our affairs.

Scripture: No one lights a lamp and hides it in a jar or puts it under a bed. Instead, he puts it on a stand, so that those who come in can see the light. For there is nothing hidden that will not be disclosed, and nothing concealed that will not be known or brought out into the open. Therefore consider carefully how you listen. Whoever has will be given more; whoever does not have, even what he thinks he has will be taken from him. (Luke 8:16–18)

I have a niece who teaches first grade in an Illinois public school. She is unable to speak openly of her faith in Christ, but she is not hindered in her ability to show her faith. Last year she had a particularly difficult class because of one boy, Jeff. Jeff had only a mom at home, and she was unable to help him with homework because she could not read. My niece was unable to communicate with the mother because they had no phone, and the notes that she sent home returned unopened.

Things would not have been so bad if Jeff had been a reasonably normal boy, but he was not. He was a severe discipline problem for the whole class. His fits were so violent that my niece had to physically restrain him to keep him from destroying the classroom and hurting himself. As she held him tightly, she would say over and over, "I love you, Jeff. You're a good boy. I love you, Jeff." She could have dumped Jeff on someone else but felt God wanted him in her class.

On the last day of school, Jeff came late. He walked to school every morning, and on this last day he picked something up along the way. He approached my niece's desk with a geranium plant behind his back, roots and all. "Here, Teacher," he said as he thrust his gift forward, "I love you too."

Lord, remind me that I can change another through my love. That's how you changed me.